Watch Out!

Insights to Discern and Overcome Evil through
the Word of God and Personal Experiences

EMMA BEACHAM

WESTBOW
PRESS®
A DIVISION OF THOMAS NELSON
& ZONDERVAN

WestBow Press books may be ordered through booksellers or by contacting:

WestBow Press
A Division of Thomas Nelson & Zondervan
1663 Liberty Drive
Bloomington, IN 47403
www.westbowpress.com
844-714-3454

ISBN: 979-8-3850-2730-9 (sc)
ISBN: 979-8-3850-2731-6 (e)

Library of Congress Control Number: 2024911992

Print information available on the last page.

WestBow Press rev. date: 07/27/2024

Stay alert! Watch out for your great enemy, the devil. He prowls around like a roaring lion, looking for someone to devour. Stand firm against him, and be strong in your faith...
1 Peter 5:8-9 NLT

CONTENTS

ACKNOWLEDGMENTS

I want to thank my children–Nichole, Melodie, Booker and Faith–for allowing me to tell some of our difficult experiences of going through dark times and receiving victories through the tender care of our Father God. Some of the problems we experienced could have been avoided if I had known better, but regardless, our Good God brought us through them all. I thank our Lord God for watching over us and causing my children to grow up to be the mighty man and mighty women who are excelling in life. You are my precious treasures, and now you're raising special treasures who are also excelling as they grow!

I also want to thank the editor of this book, Judy Walters. She was much more than an editor. She was also a spiritual advisor who checked me on certain things and caused me to think through some concepts and phrases to better present the Truth and reflect the heart of God. She was the catalyst and generous contributor who caused this book to be published.

FOREWORD

I felt honored when Emma asked me to write the foreword to her book. She is the eleventh child in our family of fifteen; I am the ninth. Our parents were sharecroppers, and education was not a main focus in our family. Most of us did not get much formal education because we were required to work on the farm for much of the school year. Emma and four other siblings were too young to work the crops of tomatoes, cabbage, peppers, cucumbers, strawberries, cotton, and sweet and white potatoes that we grew, so the older children convinced our parents to send her and the three younger ones to school where Emma learned the basics and did well in school, but she didn't have the patience to help me with my homework.

Although Emma was getting a formal education, she was not getting any help with her mental health. She earned a Bachelor's degree in Electrical Engineering from Tennessee State University, making her the first sibling to graduate from college. Then she went to Stanford University for her Master's, but lacked three hours from graduating when she left school, went to Florida and got married.

She grew up in a house with fourteen other siblings but stayed mostly to herself, harboring so much anger that when she did interact with her siblings, she would end up fighting them to the point of trying to kill them!

As the oldest of the five children left at home while our parents and other siblings were away working the crops, Emma was left in charge. Mary, five years younger than Emma, remembers a time when she wanted to get revenge for the way Emma treated them. She convinced the three other younger siblings to help her. When the time came to take action, however, the other three disappeared and Mary had to face Emma's rage alone. She leaped on Mary and scratched up her face badly. Mother was so upset with her that she gave her a good whippin'!

I remember another time when Emma, Robert, and I were in the kitchen of our home on the farm. Robert teased Emma about something she didn't like. She picked up a knife and threw it at him. Fortunately, Robert ducked, and the knife missed him. She was also very rude and disrespectful to our mother, even making her cry at times. In fact, even though mother loved her, she said that Emma was the only one of her children that she didn't miss after they left home. I asked other family members what memories of Emma they had growing up, and they all said the same thing. She was mean!

When she gave her life to Jesus, Emma changed radically. What she shares in this book are some of the ways she walked through to victory. Her desire is to teach, encourage and challenge others to overcome many of the problems resulting from difficult childhood years.

All of us–especially our mother–were grateful for the change! The weekend of our mother's funeral, Emma led Mary, Willie Mae, and me to the Lord, bringing a wonderful peace to the family. Today every one of our family members can stand together as friends!

I was her confidante and prayer partner when she went through marriage turmoil as her husband dealt with drug addiction. In spite of his addiction, all four of her children have become healthy, successful adults. God is good!

God's Word works; Emma is living proof! If God can change Emma, He can change you!

Betty Littleton
Sister

INTRODUCTION

Stay alert! Watch out for your great enemy, the devil. He prowls around like a roaring lion, looking for someone to devour. Stand firm against him, and be strong in your faith.
1 Peter 5:8-9 NLT

For over twenty years, I have been in the prayer ministry and have faced many situations and challenges to pray through on the behalf of individuals, families, ministries and businesses. However, some of the greatest challenges and life lessons that I have faced over the years have been with my own immediate family–dealing with a drug-addicted husband for 18 years (seven of those years we were separated until he passed away), being a single parent to four children, having severe financial problems, being homeless several times and other difficulties.

All of that happened after I came to know the Lord and was being delivered from childhood bondages of my father's rejection, suicidal thoughts and attempts, debilitating fear, hate, blinding rage, molestation, depression, deep insecurities with self-pity, and more. I thought it was impossible to be free–until I gave my life to Jesus and learned about our authority in His Name and the power of His Blood to make me more than a conqueror over all of it.[1]

Jesus said we have an enemy whose only purpose is to steal, kill and destroy. He also alerted us to watch and pray so we don't enter into temptation because that enemy, who is called the devil and satan, is always working to lure all of mankind into one of his traps to accomplish his agenda. He's a master of deception, and his goal is to deceive everyone. However, we are not ignorant of his wiles and intentions because our Lord and Advocate has given us insight and understanding to distinguish the difference between God's works and the enemy's works. He has also given us the tools and wisdom to stand against anything the devil throws our way and to conquer it all as He leads us to victory every time.[2]

As previously stated, I know all too well what it's like to be deceived by the devil and trapped in his snares of the many bondages I struggled with from early childhood. As a result, I grew up miserable and without hope of ever being free until I received salvation when I was 27. Then my Deliverer freed me from every bondage that once controlled my life—some instantly, but most of them over a process of growing up in the knowledge of His Word through studying it, learning from different ministries and from His Spirit.[3] During that process, I learned to recognize some of satan's snares and strategies and how to defeat him. That is why He instructed me to write this book—so I can share what I've learned to help others recognize and defeat him too.

The Lord said in Hosea 4:6, *My people are destroyed for lack of knowledge*. So I share knowledge from many years of studying the Word and overcoming experiences that have kept me and my family from being destroyed. I trust it will help others avoid suffering through some of the many mistakes that I made through ignorance or lack of watching properly.

The Lord's main charge to me from the beginning of my Christian life has been to 'overcome', and I have had many opportunities to do so over the years. Thus, my instruction for this book is to let my overcoming testimonies do the teaching, so I major on telling the experiences and resulting victories that glorify God and His faithfulness to honor His Word in my life.

I am very grateful to have found out that the answer to every conceivable problem is given to us in the Treasure of God's Word. I've learned to take His Word very seriously and apply it personally. Study it, He said. Seek Him and He will give me all that I need.[4] No weapon that my enemy forms against me can prosper and no evil will befall me. He promised![5] I believe to receive all of that and more as I honor Him and He honors me.[6] I trust you who read this book will receive what is needed to overcome your enemy as well.

1

BE WATCHFUL WITH PRAYER

Finally, my brethren, be strong in the Lord and in the power of His might. Put on the whole armor of God, that you may be able to stand against the wiles of the devil...praying always with all prayer and supplication in the Spirit, being watchful to this end with all perseverance and supplication for all the saints.
Ephesians 6:10-11,18 NKJV

I am aware that some people have the theology that God is Supreme so He's going to do whatever He wants to do, and we have no say in it because our destinies are fixed. However, even though He is Supreme, Scripture says the opposite.[7] Otherwise, there would be no need for prayer if everything is already fixed with no hope of change. It doesn't take much knowledge of the Word of God to know that prayer can change things–not change God, but change things, situations, etc.[8]

One of the greatest lessons that I learned shortly after becoming a Christian is the absolute integrity of God's Word. Believing in its infallibility is the anchor for my faith to know my prayers will be answered. I can be assured He will answer them because I pray for His will to be done according to what He has recorded in His Word that shows us Who He is and what He has made available for us.[9]

1

He gave us free will, and since we have an adversary who is vying for our loyalty through deception, we must choose whom we will serve.[10] When I choose to honor God's Word, I choose Him, and I have a right to have everything it says I should have as His child. But I have to agree with it and ask. Therefore, I pray. I pray to give God the right to stop my adversary from stealing, killing and destroying and to receive His blessings that He said are mine.

It is written in James 4:8 that when we draw close to God, He draws close to us. Our thanksgiving, praise and worship draws us close to Him.[11] I have found that in this closeness, He allows me to feel what He feels, see what He sees, and know what He knows about the things that are necessary for me to defeat the devil and be the overcomer He called me to be.

In this closeness, I feel His pleasure when He's pleased, His displeasure when He's grieved, His anger that gives me the same zeal that Jesus had to stand against unrighteousness when He cleansed the temple. I feel His compassion for the hurting and His love for all mankind. I have eyes to see and ears to hear what the Spirit is saying to me. I get insight by the Spirit on those hidden things that I need to know and some insight on what is going to happen in the future and what to do about it.[12]

TAKE AUTHORITY OVER THE ENEMY

> *Stay alert! Watch out for your great enemy, the devil. He prowls around like a roaring lion, looking for someone to devour. Stand firm against him, and be strong in your faith...* (1 Peter 5:8-9 NLT)

In October 1992, I dreamed of a lion stalking me and received the interpretation from the Lord. I had grown spiritually since giving my life to Jesus. By this time, I was walking in the love of

God and had learned a lot about how to use my authority over satan. The dream is as follows:

I was walking down a double-track dirt road with overgrown grass in between the tire paths and on each side of the road. I was in a very secluded wooded area. It was a very gloomy, late evening, and fear filled the atmosphere. I sensed eerie little demons just ahead of me. In fact, I could see visible signs of their presence as they scampered away from my approach into the overgrown grass, leaving it swaying back and forth. Hence, I could tell they greatly feared me.

In addition to the little demons scurrying about beside the pathway, I knew that I was being stalked from behind by a very large lion. I kept looking back to see him, but he always managed to hide himself from me. However, I knew he was there. I also knew I had authority over him, and that he knew it as well. That's why he was cautiously stalking me while looking for an opportunity to overtake me by surprise.

The little demons ahead of me on the pathway did not concern me. It was the big lion that concerned me because I could not see what he was up to. Although I did not fear him or the little demons, I had a constant foreboding that he would jump me from behind.

For these reasons, I kept looking behind me trying to spot the lion. Because I was constantly looking backwards, my progress along the path was greatly hindered. Also, I was constantly bracing myself, expecting to be jumped on, even though I knew I would immediately make him leave me. This resistance of fear required my full attention. Therefore, my mind was almost totally preoccupied with the enemy stalking me.

Finally, I got fed up with the torment this brought to my mind, and I stopped suddenly and turned to face him. He hid himself as before; nevertheless, I spoke to him with the authority that I knew I had over him. I commanded him to leave and not to follow me again. He left! I continued along my path without the hindrance of continually looking backwards.

Interpretation:

At the time of this dream, satan was trying to torment my mind with forebodings about our future. We were in the process of losing our home with no place to go and no money. The Lord was showing me I didn't have to put up with satan's fear tactics that I had been allowing to hinder my faith. Up to that point, I had been progressing rather slowly in building my faith for provision while at the same time I had been allowing foreboding thoughts to kill my hope of overcoming in this area. God was encouraging me to take authority over the fear that was defeating my faith to get my needs met properly. No more looking backwards while expecting more problems to overtake us!

In other words, He was telling me not to allow fear to hang in the background as a threat of failure and doom. Don't allow it to fulfill its purpose of stealing peace and destroying hope and faith. Don't let it build an expectancy of bad things happening because then satan can leap on the expectancy and cause it to come to pass. Instead, keep looking ahead and growing in faith and trust in the Lord, and all fear will lose its grip.

Since having the dream, I have had other situations where I felt pressure that I came to realize was from the enemy, and then I took my authority and rebuked him. Now I have come to be more watchful in the spirit and quicker to cut off the demonic forces that are the root cause of many problems.

DON'T RECEIVE CONDEMNATION

> *Beloved, if our heart does not condemn us, we have confidence toward God.* (1 John 3:21 NKJV)

Condemnation is a faith killer. It hinders our confidence to trust God and get prayers answered. I believe it is one of the greatest hindrances to receiving the love of God and having faith in Him and His Word to work for us on an individual basis. I know it was like that for me until I learned the Truth that when we make Jesus our Lord and Savior, God doesn't condemn us.[13] However, our own self-accusing heart and the devil (the accuser of the brethren) will indeed ruthlessly condemn us![14]

It wasn't easy for me to get delivered from the harassing, self-condemning thoughts that relentlessly flooded my mind in my early Christian life since I did not immediately get free from my ongoing habit of bashing myself whenever I made a mistake. In fact, I had to do much meditating and confessing the Word to be able to see myself as God sees me. He sees me through His Eyes of Love like I see my children, regardless of how they act. How grateful I am that I learned the Truth of His love for me. His love set me free!

A Word to the Believer from Jesus, Our Intercessor and Advocate

> *My little children, these things I write to you, so that you may not sin. And if anyone sins, we have an Advocate with the Father, Jesus Christ the righteous.* (1 John 2:1 NKJV)

Jesus, our Advocate with the Father God, spoke this Word to me in May 2022:

> *"When I came in human form, I experienced much of what you experience, without engaging in sin. I felt the pressure from the enemy. I felt the darkness all around, trying to engulf Me and take control of Me. In the Garden, I felt the anguish of soul beyond anything you can imagine, and the*

5

demonic pressure to give in to the desire of the flesh to quit My Assignment in order to get relief and avoid the horrors of death to come.[15]

Even though I never knew the battle of darkness <u>within</u> Me, I knew the strength of the battle of darkness <u>against</u> Me and against you. So I understand your weaknesses and temptations to give in to the pleasures and pressures of sin. I overcame it all for you, and I handed you My Victory so you can overcome it all too.[16]

I don't condemn you when you fall short of My Glory and give in to sin instead of overcoming it as I did; but I will judge you in the end for not taking hold of My Victory given to you through the Fruit and Gifts of the Holy Spirit and applying them to overcome your flesh and your arch enemy.[17] *You will not be held accountable for sinning but genuinely repenting of it. However, My people will be held accountable at the Judgment for neglecting and/or rejecting My commandment to love one another as I have loved you. You will be held accountable for neglecting and rejecting My Word which is the Truth that makes you free in your soul and body and in every area of your lives and families and in the lives of others that I called you to reach.*[18]

I'm at the Right Hand of Our Father interceding for you to receive all the angelic help that you need to ensure that you are free to choose without being overpowered by your enemy who is stronger than you.[19] *You cannot defeat him with your own strength. So until you learn My ways, I, the Lord of the angelic hosts,*[20] *fight for you to give you the opportunity to learn and grow through My Word and by My Spirit within you. If you fail to use what I have given you, then you allow the enemy to gain advantage over you to steal, kill and destroy. Once you grow in grace and in the knowledge of Me, your faith keeps you free as you believe, speak and do My Word.*[21]

A Word For New Believers

In November 1995, I dreamed a dream that came from God. In the dream, I stood gazing in utter fascination at an incredibly huge, lofty and barren tree with no leaves. As I gazed upon the tree, I stood in complete awe of its majestic stature and beauty, so much so that I could not take my eyes off it. In fact, I felt great respect and honor for it.

I knew in my spirit that this tree had recently been transplanted to a new location. Although I could not see its root system, I knew that as soon as it was transplanted, the roots immediately clamped tightly into the soil and began to grow in haste toward the nearest source of water. It was very clear in my spirit that this tree was very sound and wise, and it could not be held back from flourishing. Thus, I knew it would soon bear much fruit.

When I awakened, the image of that tree remained transfixed in my mind. It was very puzzling to me how I had seen the tree in the dream versus how I remembered it afterwards. In the dream I saw it as beautiful and majestic, but when I awakened and recalled the dream, I realized the tree was actually incredibly huge, barren, and ugly, and it looked absolutely dead. I asked the Lord what the dream meant, and He gave me this interpretation.

This scripture came to my mind for the dream:

...that they may be called oaks of righteousness [lofty, strong, and magnificent, distinguished for

7

> *uprightness, justice, and right standing with God],*
> *the planting of the Lord, that He may be glorified.*
> (Isaiah 61:3 AMPC)

While experiencing the dream, I was seeing from God's viewpoint. When I awoke, I was seeing through my natural eyes.

In the beginning of a new believer's life, they are like a newly transplanted tree– translated from the domain of darkness into the Kingdom of God. Although we are immediately alive to God in our spirits and He sees the beauty within us, many still look dead in the natural to observers while we are getting rooted in our new life in Christ. This is especially true for those of us who come to the Lord later in life after having lived harsh lives with lots of baggage.

The Lord showed me that because I immediately started my Christian walk with studying and doing the Word, my roots clamped into the rich soil of the Word and began to grow towards the water– the washing of the water of the Word.[22] This is beautiful to Him and it draws His honor, for He honors those who honor Him.[23]

Therefore, I encourage the new Believers–who are getting rooted and grounded in the Word and learning to walk in the Spirit and live by faith–not to receive self-condemnation or condemnation from others like I suffered in my early Christian life. The Father God gives all His children time to bear fruit.[24] In a reasonable time frame, however, He requires each one to grow in the knowledge of God and to live out what we have learned.

THE BEAUTY OF REPENTANCE

> *...You will not reject a broken and repentant heart,*
> *O God.* (Psalm 51:17 NLT)

Many years ago, the Lord instructed me to study *repentance*. So I studied Scriptures and many Biblical accounts of evil-doers repenting when they were facing judgment. In the process,

I clearly saw how tenderly God deals with people when they repent. Furthermore, I have come to understand that repentance is beautiful to Him, and He is so eager to respond to the brokenhearted with His tenderness and forgiveness, no matter how awful and evil they have been.[25]

I believe He wanted me to study this so I could grasp His heart for the repentant and better help me throw off all condemnation when I miss the mark. Also, I know He wants me to share His tenderness and love to others who struggle with condemnation even after they have repented like I once did. What's more, He wants us not to hold wrongdoings against others when they have repented.

Here are some great examples that show His heart:

King Ahab

> But there was no one like Ahab who sold himself
> to do wickedness in the sight of the Lord, because
> Jezebel his wife stirred him up. (1 Kings 25 NKJV)

When the Lord sent Elijah to Ahab to pronounce judgment on him and on Jezebel for all the evil they had done, Ahab tore his clothing, dressed in burlap, and fasted. He even slept in burlap and softened his attitude. Then the Lord said to Elijah, *"Do you see how Ahab has humbled himself before me? Because he has done this, I will not do what I promised during his lifetime..."* (1 Kings 21:17-29 NLT)

King Manasseh

> ...Manasseh led them to do even more evil than the
> pagan nations that the Lord had destroyed when the
> people of Israel entered the land. Then the Lord said
> through his servants the prophets: "King Manasseh
> of Judah has done many detestable things. He is

> *even more wicked than the Amorites, who lived in*
> *this land before Israel. He has caused the people of*
> *Judah to sin with his idols.* (2 Kings 21:9-11 NLT)

King Manasseh is one of the best examples I know in the Bible of an evil-bent, darkened heart turning to God in genuine repentance and having good works to show it.

He had built altars and places of worship for many idols, worshiped them, and had turned his people against God while leading them to worship his idols as well. He also practiced much witchcraft and even burned up his own children in sacrifice to his idols.

When the Lord spoke to Manasseh and the Israelites who had followed him into sin against God, they ignored His warnings. So He sent the captains of the Assyrian army against him. They took Manasseh prisoner, bound him in chains and took him to Babylon[26] where Manasseh repented and received God's remarkable mercy and forgiveness:

> *But while in deep distress, Manasseh sought the Lord*
> *his God and sincerely humbled himself before the*
> *God of his ancestors. And when he prayed, the Lord*
> *listened to him and was moved by his request. So*
> *the Lord brought Manasseh back to Jerusalem and*
> *to his kingdom. Then Manasseh finally realized that*
> *the Lord alone is God!* (2 Chronicles 33:12-13 NLT)

After that, Manasseh rebuilt the outer wall of the City of David. He also removed the foreign gods and the idol from the Lord's Temple, and he tore down all the pagan altars he had built. Then he restored the altar of the Lord and sacrificed peace and thanksgiving offerings on it. He also encouraged the people he had once led astray to worship the Lord again.[27]

King Hezekiah

There is also the account of Hezekiah whom God told to get his house in order because he was going to die. He responded by turning his face to the wall and deeply repenting. God gave him 15 more years to live.[28]

City of Nineveh

Another great account of God's mercy to forgive is when He forgave the whole city of Nineveh when they all fasted and repented of their wickedness after Jonah delivered God's Word of judgment to them. God reversed the judgment and didn't destroy the city.[29]

Seven Churches of Revelation

In His letters to six of the seven churches in Revelation, the Lord Jesus rebuked them for their sins, corrected them and admonished them to repent so He would not have to judge them.[30]

In calling my attention to know His heart for the repentant, He dealt with me about His patience to give everyone time to repent while instructing me to do the same. In the light of His readiness to forgive, He reiterated to me the dangers of judging other Christians for their past sins (that do not involve me personally) because they may have repented to Him, been cleansed and found favor in His sight. Therefore, if I judge them based on what I have heard or assumed, I would be found guilty of falsely accusing my brother, thus bringing judgment upon myself.[31]

On a personal note, Jesus told us to:

Take heed to yourselves. If your brother sins against you, rebuke him; and if he repents, forgive him. And if he sins against you seven times in a day,

> *and seven times in a day returns to you, saying, 'I repent,' you shall forgive him."* (Luke 17:3-4 NKJV)

He freely forgives the repentant, and He requires us to do the same.

DON'T LET TROUBLE TROUBLE YOU

> *Peace I leave with you; My [perfect] peace I give to you; not as the world gives do I give to you. Do not let your heart be troubled, nor let it be afraid. [Let My perfect peace calm you in every circumstance and give you courage and strength for every challenge.]* (John 14:27 AMP)

The Lord gave me the title above after I was told that a good friend had been in an accident, possibly with children involved. I first had to calm myself so I would not allow emotional trauma and fear to control me. Then I prayed for the situation. I had to continue to resist the fear that pressured my mind with negative thoughts. Once I got alone, I began to practice what I have learned to do when trouble comes. I started praising the Lord with faith that He will intervene and cause everything to work out. Perfect peace rose up in my heart. That's when He spoke the phrase to me, *"Don't let trouble trouble you."* This brought to my mind other Words and Scriptures that He has given me in the past for troubling situations.

While resisting fear regarding all the frightening concerns about Y2K, I almost panicked with others and thought about stocking up on items like they were doing. Since I didn't have much extra money to buy for future needs, I asked the Lord if I needed to store up some water, etc. He said no, and the temptation to fret over what bad things might happen at the start of the year

2000 was quenched. His answer reassured me that no matter what, He would take care of our needs.

On September 11, 2001, the infamous day of 9/11, I was at work, with no outside communication other than occasional updates via phone calls relaying the tragedies that were unfolding. We were told that gas prices were skyrocketing because of the attacks. When we finally left work that afternoon, sure enough, there were greatly inflated prices and ridiculously long lines at every gas station that I passed, except one who had the longest lines because their prices remained the same. My co-worker, who was driving in front of me, called and said she was getting gas there before they raised their prices too. So she got in line and I pulled in behind her.

After a few minutes, the Lord told me to get out of line and go home. In my fear of prices going higher, I tried to reason with Him that I should fill up to be on the safe side. He repeated the instruction, and I got out of line and went home. After about two hours of watching the news about the attack, He told me to go get gas on 31st street (earlier I had been on 41st). To my surprise, when I went to the same gas franchise, it was business as usual, with no gas hike, no lines and no panic. I assumed things had calmed down and were basically back to normal elsewhere in the city.

After I filled up and was on the way home, He spoke to my heart, *"Don't ever panic with the world. Trust Me!"* A short while later, I found out things were not back to normal when my daughter came home from school and informed me that just several blocks away gas lines were wrapped into the streets. I was very grateful that God had led me away from all the worry and panic earlier while I waited in a long line unnecessarily. Instead, He led me to a place of peace right in the midst of all the chaos.

That experience clearly showed me how the Lord can set us apart from the troubles of this world when we put our trust in Him and allow Him to lead us to victory. Since then, whenever alarming threats or troubling situations arise in the world, I am reminded of the

Word God spoke to me that day, and it helps me to resist fear and stay calm while I trust Him to guide and protect me and my loved ones.

In 2011, I faced another troubling situation with my daughter and her car. While praying about it, the Lord said, *"It's not as bad as it seems."* He went on to tell me that when I involve Him and keep my peace and joy, I can always say that. Why? Because He won't allow the situation to go to the depth of where it would go without Him, but He will turn things around. That is a personal Word which will work for anyone. However, He made it clear that prayer and obedience to His instructions, which puts us in harmony with His will and leads us to victory, is essential for us to allow Him to act on our behalf.[32] I now speak this phrase in every negative situation and watch Him turn bad things to good, over and over again. It's not as bad as it seems!

Later on, He showed me the Scripture that confirms this Word:

> *I have told you these things, so that in Me you may have [perfect] peace and confidence. In the world you have tribulation and trials and distress and frustration; but be of good cheer [take courage; be confident, certain, undaunted]! For I have overcome the world. [I have deprived it of power to harm you and have conquered it for you.]* (John 16:33 AMPC)

To sum it all up: Jesus overcame every trouble that we'll ever face; and as we receive His victory that He won for us, we'll always win. Although we can't keep trouble from coming our way, with our God's help, we can always conquer it and get victory in the end.

MEDITATE ON THE WORD

> *Study this Book of Instruction continually. Meditate on it day and night so you will be sure to obey*

*everything written in it. Only then will you prosper
and succeed in all you do.* (Joshua 1:8 NLT)

The Lord spoke to my heart in June 2018:

> *"Meditation is about extended focus on the Word,
> Instruction or Teaching so that you can retain the
> memory, gain insight, and receive wisdom and
> understanding from the Lord."*

Later, He made it clear that it is necessary to meditate on the Word long enough to allow the Holy Spirit to open up the understanding so I can fully comprehend that Truth and be rid of all doubt.

One of the first things about which the Lord dealt with me after I gave my life to Him was to stop worrying and instead to give my concerns to Him in prayer! That was not easy for me because I grew up being a champion worrier, and letting go of my bad habit was no simple task.

I was greatly disturbed when I first came across the Scripture in Philippians telling us not to worry[33] because I thought I couldn't do it. Praying instead of worrying is a very attractive concept, but I couldn't see myself living that way. My habit was just too strongly embedded in my soul for it to be that simple!

Even though I tried to move on and study something else, I was impressed to go back to that same Scripture every day to read it and think about it. I was a new Believer, and at the time, I didn't know the Lord was leading me to meditate on that Scripture until my mind was renewed enough to accept it and my heart could truly believe it. This went on for many days until one day I had a literal experience of that Word dropping down from my head into my heart. Reading and meditating on that Scripture over and over had reframed my thinking and freed me! From then on, it was very practical and doable.

I can now resist worry and believe God to take care of it all.

Through that experience, the Lord showed me how to destroy any negative thought pattern and take any part of the Word from mere head knowledge to heart knowledge so I can pray it in faith, without doubt, and receive the blessings of His promises.

HAVE A VICTOR MENTALITY

> *Yet even in the midst of all these things, we triumph over them all, for God has made us to be more than conquerors, and his demonstrated love is our glorious victory over everything!* (Romans 8:37 TPT)

In one of the prayer groups I attended, before we would pray our leader often spent a short time sharing Biblical wisdom for effective prayer. One day she taught along these lines: When Jesus rose from the dead, He handed us His victory over satan and all his evil works against us. So in His eyes we (everyone who receives Him as Lord) have access to everything we need to live a victorious life. Because His victory is already given to us, we receive it by faith. We don't beg God or struggle to get it. We must protect what the enemy is trying to steal. We must see ourselves as victors sitting above the problem and looking down on it rather than as victims underneath the burden of it, she explained.[34]

I had heard teaching along this line before and was practicing it in part, but that day I was able to take it to another level. I had been fairly strong in using this viewpoint in healing the body since the time I finally got the revelation that God calls us healed through the price Jesus paid at the whipping post. Therefore, I treat sickness as an invasion against myself and others for whom I pray, and I stand against it with the Word of God that says we are healed.[35] Consequently, we receive healings often. However, I often fell short in receiving answers in other areas until I grasped this Truth and put it into daily practice in my thoughts, my words and my actions.

I have been a part of many prayer groups and personal prayer sessions, and I have learned the necessity of keeping the right attitude by focusing on the answer and not the problem, especially when facing a serious matter. I personally learned that anxious prayers that are focused on the problem are faithless prayers, and they do not connect with God. Therefore, I gladly received God's instruction to never accept being a victim again. Instead, at all times I'll keep my eyes fixed on my Victor and His victory that He won for us so that my prayers will always be filled with the faith that pleases God, and I'll receive the reward of the answers I seek. I now see myself as a victorious overcomer through His victory, and I consistently get victorious results.[36]

PRAY WITH KNOWLEDGE AND WISDOM

> *For the Lord gives wisdom; From His mouth come knowledge and understanding;* (Proverbs 2:6 NKJV)

After studying and meditating on the Word of God and developing a victor mentality based on His promises and His victories that He has accomplished for us, then we are ready to appropriately pray according to His will and receive answers to our prayers.

Over the years, I have witnessed many Christians who have no confidence that their prayers will be answered. It's easily seen that one major reason is a lack of knowledge of what the Word of God says regarding their situation and, therefore, a lack of understanding on how to pray specifically. Another reason is a lack of faith because of no specific Scripture(s) on which to base their prayer. That's because Biblical faith only comes from hearing the Word–not just hearing with the outer ear but hearing with the heart as the Holy Spirit speaks revelation to our spirit when we spend appropriate time seeking and listening to Him.[37]

I personally know that just throwing out a quick prayer with no Scriptural basis and then getting no answer can really hinder one's faith, especially if done too often. It helps to learn this early in our Christian walk so we won't give up on truly expecting answers to our prayers.

It's also good for us to understand that the Father has provided everything we could possibly need in our Covenant with Him, but we must access the Covenant promises through our faith.[38] He states in 2 Peter 1:3-4 NKJV:

> *...His divine power has given to us all things that pertain to life and godliness*, *through the knowledge of Him who called us by glory and virtue, by which have been given to us exceedingly great and precious promises, that through these you may be partakers of the divine nature, having escaped the corruption that is in the world through lust.*

Although these promises are ours through our Lord Jesus, God requires us to come to Him and access them based on the protocols He laid out for us in His Word. That is, He requires everyone who approaches Him to believe that He rewards those who sincerely seek him.[39] Other protocols require us to pray to the Father in Jesus' Name,[40] to ask in faith while fully expecting without doubt to receive the answer,[41] and to have corresponding action with our prayer.[42] In line with these protocols, first of all we must approach Him with thanksgiving and praise, believing He is good and His mercy is everlasting to us. This honors Him in His place as our God who made us.[43] Jesus taught us to give God this acknowledgment and honor at the beginning and ending of what we call the Lord's Prayer.[44]

God said He has already answered yes to all His promises in Jesus, and through Jesus we say Amen (in trust and acceptance) to receive them.[45] So that's why He expects us to come to Him with thanksgiving as we trust Him to do what He promised. With that understanding, when I pray, I don't try to produce an answer, or convince God that my prayer should be answered or beg God to help me. I simply receive what He has already promised and provided in His Word. Wisdom, however, is needed on how to pray effectively, and the Holy Spirit gives us that wisdom when we ask Him.[46] I learned that is why it is so important to take time to listen and get His take on things. My faith is solidified when I hear, in my heart, His wisdom and guidance on how to deal with the matter according to His Word.

My confidence in getting prayers answered comes from praying the Word (the Scriptures and what God speaks to my heart) that gives the answers to my situation. In other words, I return His Word back to Him so He can answer it and cause it to prosper on my behalf. I can fully trust Him to do what He has promised because He said He watches over His Word to perform it.[47] Therefore, I often start my prayers with, "Lord, You said…." I seal my prayers with the authority in Jesus' Name, and then I thank Him in advance.

Many years ago, my pastor changed my prayer life when He taught that we need to go to the Lord to get wisdom on HOW to pray about a matter before we actually pray. This is how I have had success in praying for myself and my children for many years, especially when dealing with healing. I seek Him for direction in order to target the root cause. Some causes are natural, some nutritional, some environmental or spiritual. God's Word that brings us healing covers all causes; however, our approach on how to pray and receive the healing may be different.

we need to go to the Lord to get wisdom on HOW to pray about a matter before we actually pray.

This is also true when praying for anything. Some issues stem from natural occurrences and some are demonically driven. It takes discernment from God to know the difference, and He invites us to ask for the wisdom we need for it is His good pleasure to give us everything in His kingdom.[48]

STAY IN FAITH AND DON'T DOUBT

> *Only it must be in faith that he asks with no wavering (no hesitating, no doubting). For the one who wavers (hesitates, doubts) is like the billowing surge out at sea that is blown hither and thither and tossed by the wind. For truly, let not such a person imagine that he will receive anything [he asks for] from the Lord,* (James 1:6-7 AMPC)

The Lord once spoke to my heart, "Let the Word you're standing on fight for you." In line with this, we're told to fight the good fight of faith. This kind of faith comes from hearing and believing the Word.[49]

"Let the Word you're standing on fight for you."

My early years of walking with God were not without challenges. Although I acknowledged the integrity of God's Word and I believed all of it is true, that didn't keep me from struggling to receive some things it promises. I did trust Him, but when it came to those certain things where there appeared to be no viable solution, I often failed to receive an answer to my prayers. I had long ago decided to believe all of the Word, so my question was, "Why was I failing to receive answers when I needed them the most?"

I soon learned that, although the Word is perfect, I had to allow the Word to work in me so I could be able to receive and experience what it says. I was eventually shown that the Word never failed me, but I often failed it with my weak, undeveloped faith. Not seeing how it could work for me was my biggest barrier to receiving answers. I had too many 'if's' and 'but's' in my self-abased thinking to allow the Word to work for me personally in certain areas.

So the Lord taught me to keep my focus on the promised Word and not to be moved by anything that suggests it won't work for me. This is where the 'fight of faith' comes into play. In order to keep my focus on the answer and off the problem, I have to fight doubt and fear of failure, and the only weapon that can defeat those enemies is the Word of God. I have learned that when we take our stand and don't waver, it's a good fight because one way or another we always win.

This is also true when it comes to personal Words from the Lord. Our relationship with God is very personal, and I've found that it really pleases Him when we come to Him to get His personal instructions on how to fix a situation instead of doing things the world's way. I have had many occasions when I needed a specific Word from the Lord to give us victory in a situation. One of my most memorable ones is when my teenage daughter received an unjust traffic ticket.

We were just about to leave our apartment complex to take the kids to school when a school bus stopped near our main entrance close to where we lived. Instead of waiting, we traveled through the complex to exit further down the street where we could bypass the bus. We had only gone a little distance when a police officer came after us. He stopped us and gave my daughter a ticket. I suppose he had seen us in the complex near the main entrance, then a few minutes later he looked up and saw us on the street. We tried to explain how we exited, but he wouldn't listen. Instead, he insisted that we had passed the bus.

This was very troubling, not only because it was an unjust ticket, but also because teenagers and tickets are a bad combination when it comes to insurance rates. I admit, we were upset at first, but we calmed down and forgave the officer because he believed he was right, and it was his duty to give the ticket. However, we resolved to fight it. Only I knew we had to fight it in the spirit before we went to court. So I went to our God of Justice for help, asking Him for wisdom on how to go about dealing with the injustice and getting the ticket dismissed. Then He gave us the answer for victory.

Instead of praying anymore about it, He said to proclaim, *"The charges are dropped!"* I told my daughter what the Lord said for us to do. Then I wrote that word on the ticket and put it on the wall where we would see it often. We would speak it out when we passed by. We had about two weeks before the court date, and we were consistent in speaking our faith. In the meantime, we prepared our defense for court by mapping the route we took to exit the apartment complex.

I must admit it didn't look promising. We had to fight a lot of doubt, but day after day we kept at it. As the court date approached, the pressures of doubt-filled thoughts coming against my mind increased, but I knew that was a normal tactic of the enemy and I didn't let up. To our joy, the day before our court date, I received a call informing us that the officer had dropped the charges. Wow! We praised our God of Justice! We were excited and grateful! Even though it's a small town, that was a total surprise, for we expected the judge to drop the charges when we went to court. I'm so glad we let our Lord handle it instead of giving in and accepting the injustice.

TARGET THE REAL ENEMY

Wear the full armor of God. Wear God's armor so that you can fight against the devil's clever tricks. Our fight is not against people on earth. We are

*fighting against the rulers and authorities and the
powers of this world's darkness. We are fighting
against the spiritual powers of evil in the heavenly
places.* (Ephesians 6:11-12 ERV)

One day when I was whining to the Lord about how badly my husband was treating me, He said, *"Your husband is not your enemy."* Really? He sure acts like it! God went on to tell me that I needed to focus my anger towards defeating my real enemy. Well, I know who that is—satan, aka the devil, the deceiver, and the father of lies. He's the one who was trying to steal our joy and peace, kill our love for one another and destroy our marriage and our lives.[50] So far, at that time, the devil was succeeding because I wasn't resisting him as much as I was resisting my husband.

I took to heart what the Lord said that day, and I started looking at the situations that arose and at my husband differently. I began looking beyond his wrongdoings and focused on who was pushing his buttons. I then took my faith and began resisting the puppeteer instead of the puppet. I also turned the spotlight on myself and worked on overcoming more of my weaknesses and not allowing my buttons to be pushed so that I would no longer be a secondary puppet in the devil's hands.

> *I then took my faith and began resisting the puppeteer instead of the puppet.*

Life changed at that point. The anger towards my husband was aimed towards my real enemy, and I no longer saw my husband as the opposition, even though his behavior towards me remained the same. With my new focus, I could see things from God's viewpoint which made me even angrier at the devil. At the same time, the compassion of God rose up in me for my husband because of how he was allowing his arch enemy to control (and even ruin) his life and business. This caused me to take my eyes off myself and consider how his behavior was negatively affecting his future. With that new insight, my prayers for my husband changed and came against my real enemy. I could then obey God's commandment better to love him with the love of God in me. Since faith works by love,[51] my prayers for God to help him could then be answered. My prayers for the Lord to protect me and the children from the darkness he was embracing were answered. Everything didn't straighten out immediately and some things never did, but even so, that change in me put me on the road to personal victory.

DON'T ACCEPT HEAVY BURDENS

> *Then Jesus said, "Come to me, all of you who are weary and carry heavy burdens, and I will give you rest. Take my yoke upon you. Let me teach you, because I am humble and gentle at heart, and you will find rest for your souls. For my yoke is easy to bear, and the burden I give you is light."* (Matthew 11:28-30 NLT)

For years I would receive alerts from the Lord with anxiousness and as a heavy burden. Then I would go into desperate seeking and praying to avert what evil the enemy intended. However, the Lord intervened one day and showed me that in the area of prayer, His burden is not heavy but light. It's a call to pray or to act on an instruction that rests upon us with a tug on the heart (sometimes a very strong tug), but any heavy oppression against the mind and emotions does not come from Him. It comes from the enemy who involves himself to bring fear and fretful doubt. He's the one who brings the pressure to try and make me feel like a big load is put upon me to pray through to victory, and many times I took the bait and labored through under the heaviness.

I learned my prayers should respond to the Lord's call with a victory mentality in order to receive the answer He wants to give! Now that I understand this Truth, I respond to His tugs with confident assurance of good results because now I know that He who initiated the prayer also empowers me to pray and intends to give the victory.

In the light of my new insight into the deceptive technique of the enemy (as well as letting my imagination run wild) when I sense a strong leading to pray, it is very liberating to get instruction from Him regarding how to handle His alerts to pray and seek Him. He said to me:

> *"Don't accept any heavy burdens. Whenever a burdensome feeling comes upon you and you 'feel' that something is wrong, you know it's either Me alerting you to seek wisdom through prayer or quiet focus, or it's the enemy of your soul trying to pull you down. I never pull you down; I just alert you. Then you sense the urgency and take it as a burden to carry. If it's the enemy, resist him with the Word. If it is Me alerting you, then rejoice that I'm leading you and do not be disturbed. Just follow the leading to the victory."*

I received that word; then I asked the Lord why do I, and other people that I have observed, typically take His leading as a heavy burden?

> *"It's because you think I alerted you so that you can fix it by praying it through,"* He responded. *"So you take it as a care and put yourself under pressure, and satan accommodates you with his oppression added to My call to pray,"* He went on to say, *"Keep all your cares cast upon Me as you take my alerts to pray, and seek Me as 'Love' speaking to you. Your response should always be with the attitude of imminent victory, knowing I've already fixed it for you. Yes, I call you to pray through to victory, but*

your prayer is to receive the victory that is already won for you, while you resist your opposition that is trying to steal from, kill, and destroy you. Always keep in mind you are receiving your victory and not producing it. Keep the pressure on Me and My Word and off yourself. Accept the call, but resist all oppressive heaviness."

> *Always keep in mind you are receiving your victory and not producing it.*

WORSHIP GOD WITH THE WHOLE HEART

Jesus said to him, "'You shall love the Lord your God with all your heart, with all your soul, and with all your mind.' This is the first and great commandment..." (Matthew 22:37-38 NKJV)

The collective definitions for worship in the Old and New Testament are summed up in outward expressions of physical bowing and prostration in honor to God, including lifting the hands in adoration to Him. Additionally, and most importantly, worship is an attitude of the heart that is bowed in total reverence and submission to God. When the heart is bowed in worship, we are close to Him and He to us. In this position, we experience His Presence where there is fullness of joy.[52]

The best example I know of someone who worshiped God with his whole heart was the shepherd boy, known as the sweet psalmist of Israel, who was eventually appointed king. The Lord Himself called David, *"...a man after My own heart, who will do all My will."*[53]

Through my studies and experience with the Lord, I believe that when we have a heart of absolute reverence and worship for

God, we will be so grateful to Him that our mouths will be filled with praise continually. This was certainly true of David, for he wrote:

> *My mouth shall be filled with Your praise and with Your honor all the day...I will hope continually, and will praise You yet more and more...My mouth shall tell of Your righteous acts and of Your deeds of salvation all the day, for their number is more than I know.* (Psalm 71:8,14,15 AMPC)

During our praise and worship service in church one Sunday morning, the Lord spoke to my heart:

> *"Whenever someone stops worshiping the Lord, they enter into a spiritual parallel of Lucifer becoming satan. Criticism, self-centeredness, ungratefulness, and finally rebellion will result if there is not a turn around."*

Another time in January 2020, He said, *"If you don't honor Me, you'll honor My enemy."* The Apostle Paul warned about the fate of those who know about God but do not honor Him. He wrote that God's wrath is against them, *"because, although they knew God, they did not glorify Him as God, nor were thankful, but became futile in their thoughts, and their foolish hearts were darkened."* (Romans 1:21 NKJV)

The Israelites proved over and over that when they did not give praise and honor to the Lord God, they ended up worshiping demonic idols instead. It has been preached and it's clearly seen that it is the same today as it was back then. I have personally witnessed some who once honored God in their lives turn away from Him to give themselves over to other things that oppose His Word. Either we will praise and honor our God, or we will

Emma Beacham

substitute an idol and worship it. The idols may be different, but the end results are the same.[54]

CLOSE THE DOOR ON THE ENEMY

Don't give the devil any opportunity to work.
(Ephesians 4:27 GW)

There were times when healing for my children could not take place until the enemy that caused it was evicted.[55] Violating the New Testament commandment to love one another is one way the door was opened to enable our enemy to torment with sickness.[56]

In August 1998, my fourteen-year-old daughter came to my bed around 5:00 a.m. with a terribly painful stomachache and sore throat. I prayed for her with no relief. I then sensed that she needed to repent for her disrespectful responses to me earlier. She repented, and I commanded the stomachache to go, and it left.

In June 2000, my nine-year-old daughter came to me at bedtime with a stomachache. I laid my hands on her intending to pray but discerned she needed to apologize to someone. I asked her if she knew who it was, and she said no. So we prayed together, and afterwards she knew she needed to apologize to her sister. She went and did so, and the stomachache left immediately without any further prayer.

We also found out through experience that some recurring sicknesses and other problems that keep returning are due to the tormentor who has been given a place.[57] Even after evicting him, because the opening through which he entered was not closed, he came right back and made things worse. One of my daughters discovered this the hard way.

At 12 years old, my second daughter had a bad stomachache when we got home from church. We prayed, and it left her. The next day it came back. We prayed and it left again. It came back worse later that night, and she suddenly and violently vomited all over my rug. Then I could see that this was serious. I knew we needed to get to the bottom of it, so I set everything aside and gave full focus to the Lord for an answer. "Lord, why isn't she getting free from this?"

He said to my heart, *"She read the horoscope."*

"You read the horoscope?" I questioned her.

Surprised and somewhat nervous, she told me it was a school assignment about reading the newspaper. I wasn't certain about how much she knew about the occult nature of the horoscope and that it opens the door to the devil and his cohorts, but we dealt with that.[58] She was remorseful and repentant, and the sickness left and never returned.

Later she confessed to me that she 'kinda' knew it was wrong, but she didn't dispute the assignment, and she actually read more than what was required. In fact, she said she was a bit intrigued by it. Therefore, the teacher set the conditions for my daughter's attack, but she drew the enemy to herself when she embraced it and went beyond the assignment. Therefore, I believe it was her intrigue that gave the enemy the occasion to attack her body. The good part is that she said she really learned a lesson not to mess with the occult.

In August 2009, the same daughter, who was then married and pregnant, called with a terrible toothache. I prayed for the pain to go; then we praised the Lord for delivering her from it and the pain left. She was kept pain free until she got to the dentist. A few weeks later she called around 2 a.m. crying because of an infectious pain in her ear. I prayed and the pain left. Three days later it came back. I prayed again; we praised God together and it left. She got medicine from the doctor, and it worked for a little while and then stopped working. The pain returned, and I prayed; we praised, and the pain left. This repeated several more times. She got stronger medicine. It worked for a while and then stopped working as before. Finally, I felt impressed to visit her over the Labor Day weekend. My thoughts were to lay hands on her and pray. So my youngest daughter and I made the 600-mile trip to deal with it in person–for her and for the baby's sake. (I was concerned about stronger meds hurting the baby.)

After traveling a short while and praying as we went, the Holy Spirit spoke to my heart that the evil spirit causing the pain had left her. I believe it left so suddenly because it didn't want to face direct opposition. That proved to be true, for when we arrived, she was doing well. She had a doctor's appointment that morning and the diagnosis was good with no more redness in ear and throat. She told me that when she got up that morning she was in great pain, but suddenly, she got better. So we just enjoyed a fun weekend visit.

I observed during our visit that my daughter and her husband were having some issues with strife, and she was dealing with unforgiveness. As this was disclosed, the Lord revealed to me and then used me to help her understand that strife was the doorway through which a 'spirit of infirmity' kept returning every time we kicked it out. That's why He sent me to go to her to help uncover the root issue. She recognized and addressed the problem by forgiving her husband. Afterwards, she had no more problems with pain.

PRAYER AND FASTING

> ...*His disciples asked Him privately, "Why could we not cast it out?" So He said to them, "This kind can come out by nothing but prayer and fasting."* (Mark 9:28-29 NKJV)

It is understood that anything we consistently feed will get stronger and what we starve will get weaker. It's the same principle with feeding our spirit with God's Word or feeding our soul with information and entertainment or the body with food.

There have been a number of times when the Lord led me to fast and dedicate more time to prayer and the Word so I would be spiritually prepared to deal with an ongoing or upcoming problem. Fasting allows me to put more focus on God, whether I'm depriving myself of food, TV or social media. Fasting weakens my affection for the thing that competes with feeding myself spiritually. While weakening the control of the flesh through fasting and at the same time strengthening my spirit through communion with the Lord in prayer and study, amazing things have resulted!

Fasting weakens my affection for the thing that competes with feeding myself spiritually.

The Word of God makes it clear that our level of spiritual strength is important when dealing with demonic forces. In years past, I have experienced times when I was not spiritually strong enough to deal with a demonic enemy, and I needed to retreat and get myself built up with the Word and prayer.[59] Now that I have a daily routine of time with the Lord and His Word (as long as I stay alert to heed His instructions), He prepares me to win every battle.

Many years ago, when my children were young, my son reacted badly to my correction and stormed out of my room with a bad attitude. Shortly, his older sister yelled from the other room that he had passed out, and she dragged him back into the room. I thought he was putting on an act and simply ignored him until the Lord spoke to my heart that it was a serious matter. I quickly ran to him; and when I looked at his face, I saw he was completely listless with his eyes rolled back in his head. I recognized the enemy had taken hold of him in his rebellious state.

I made everyone leave the room and sought the Lord for

direction as it was a strong demonic force that had him. I was utterly surprised when He told me something He had never spoken to me before or since. He said, *"This kind only comes out through prayer and fasting."* Upon hearing that, fear almost gripped my heart until I recalled and exclaimed, "I'm on a fast!" He let me know that my obedience to follow His instructions to fast is why I was prepared to cast it out. Then I used my authority in the Name of Jesus and with the Word of God commanded the demonic force to leave my child, and it did! Praise the Lord!

Over two weeks earlier, the Lord had told me to fast solid food for a length of time. I was on the eighteenth day of that fast. In hindsight, I realize that He had prepared me for what He knew would come about with my child. That spirit left because I followed God's instructions to subdue my flesh and get spiritually prepared through spending time to strengthen my inner self. This is no doubt how I was able to stay calm, reject fear and effectively use my God-given authority over it. I am so glad I obeyed!

SECURE IT IN THE SPIRIT

> *…I know whom I have believed and am persuaded that He is able to keep what I have committed to Him until that Day.* (2 Timothy 1:12 NKJV)

My husband and I had a landscaping business that went from flourishing to almost nothing due to his drug addiction. When we first separated, he was so bound with drugs that his word was not trustworthy. Whenever he promised to send us money, he never fulfilled his promise. Therefore, to give him time to get himself together and stop disappointing the children, we released him from his responsibility to support us.

However, the time came when I felt he was sincere when he made a promise, but he still didn't come through because, he said, he didn't get his full pay from the contractor or homeowner, or for some other reason. This happened multiple times over the years. Then in February 2008, the Lord gave me insight on what to do about it. He told me to receive the promised money by faith that he would keep his word. Then, by pleading the Blood of Jesus over the promise to seal the gift, I will *secure it in the spirit* to keep the devil from interfering in any way–either against my husband's business or against the contractor/homeowner who paid him.

It worked because he started following through with his promises! Praise God!

Years later, the Lord reminded me of the need to secure legitimate promises made between individuals–even in business deals–when my son-in-law and daughter got into real estate. It became clear that it was wise to use this wisdom with earnest offers under contract on their homes up for sale. One home was under contract for several months while the buyer was getting approved for the loan. Although it looked like a sure thing, it fell through. Unfortunately, by that time interest rates had increased.

Therefore, I've learned that no matter how certain something looks, always keep in mind that the enemy works day and night looking for ways to steal, kill and destroy everything he can, even 'sure things.' So I'm making it a priority to stay alert and be proactive to keep him in check and not allow him to interfere with my blessings.[60]

LISTEN CAREFULLY

I am listening carefully to all the Lord is saying—for he speaks peace to his people, his saints...(Psalm 85:8 TLB)

I am convinced that in both stages of our lives–before and

after we receive salvation–God is attempting to reveal Himself to us, to guide us and help us in some way. At a young age, before I was Born Again, He clearly told me to stop attempting to commit suicide. He told me if I did it, I'd be lost for eternity. When I was 26 years old, He spoke to me again while I was in the process of committing suicide by overdosing on 71 sleeping pills. Just before my body was completely immobilized by the poison and I was about to pass out, an extremely loud ringing tone sounded in my left ear and startled me out of my relaxed state. This happened three times as I was drifting off to sleep. The third time it rang, I sat up and exclaimed, "I don't want to die!" At that moment, I believe I experienced:

> *The word from heaven will come to us with dazzling light to shine upon those who live in darkness, near death's dark shadow. And he will illuminate the path that leads to the way of peace."*
> (Luke 1:79 TPT)

My spiritual eyes were opened, and fear gripped me. I became aware of the eternal horror toward which I was heading, and I decided I wanted to live! Then, in my befuddled state of mind, I distinctly heard God say, "*Dial 911.*" At that point, my vision was so blurred that I could barely distinguish the numbers on the phone. My hands were so weak that I barely had enough strength to dial the numbers, and my speech was so slurred the operator had difficulty understanding me. By the goodness of God, I had just enough strength left in my legs to stumble to the door to let the paramedics in when they arrived.

After 10 days in the psychiatric ward of the hospital–enduring the torment of the evil spirits that filled that place–the prayers of family and friends helped me to recover, and I was released. A short time later, I received Jesus as my Lord and Savior in my pastor's office. Then I started learning God's Word and Ways, including how to recognize, listen and be led by the Spirit of God who had come to dwell in me. I was excited to learn that Jesus sent the Holy Spirit to be our Helper. He said He will guide us into all Truth, and He will speak to us and tell us things about the future. Romans 8:14 says all Children of God are led by the Spirit of God. I was taught to listen and expect Him to speak to me as I read the Bible, pray and meditate on the Word. Then write down what I hear in my heart and follow any instructions given.

I learned that we must draw close to God to fellowship with Him, experience His Presence and hear His gentle Voice. We are told in the Psalms to come into God's Presence with thanksgiving. We are also told in the Psalms that He inhabits our praises. So one key way to draw close to Him and experience His Presence is through thanksgiving and praise.

If I have a problem sensing God's Presence and hearing His Voice, I learned I am most likely lacking the proper protocol of thanking and praising Him. Since He looks at and judges our hearts, a grateful heart expressing thanksgiving and praise to Him is necessary to approach Him properly so I can have sweet fellowship with Him.

Because He dwells in us, He guides us from within–through giving us a spiritual impression, a perception, a knowing or through speaking to us. Therefore, when I share what He speaks to me, I often say, "The Lord spoke to my heart…" There are also Biblical accounts and present-day testimonies of angels delivering messages to people. Also, some have testified that they heard the audible Voice of God. However, He has always led me from within.

Jesus said the Holy Spirit will only speak what He hears, and He will always honor and glorify Jesus. Therefore, I test the spirit that speaks to me by making certain Jesus is honored–in His Sacrifice for us, His defeat of satan, in His Lordship and His finished work that redeemed us from all the curse. This test is very necessary because we are instructed to test every spirit to see if it is the Spirit of God or a false spirit.

Hebrews 12:25 ERV says, *Be careful and don't refuse to listen when God speaks... Now God is speaking from heaven.* I believe just as an attentive earthly father regularly speaks to his little children, our God is regularly speaking to us.

In addition, Jesus said in John 14:23 NKJV, *"If anyone loves Me, he will keep My word; and My Father will love him, and We will come to him and make Our home with him..."*

Therefore, I believe (through learning from others and from my own studies) we have the Godhead–The Father, Son, and Holy Spirit–making their home in us and speaking to us through the Spirit. As a result, the Spirit witnesses to our spirit and assures us we are Children of God. His witness gives us peace. I believe this is the peace that Jesus, the Lord of Peace, promised to give us when He said:

> *"Peace I leave with you, My peace I give to you; not as the world gives do I give to you. Let not your heart be troubled, neither let it be afraid."* (John 14:27 NKJV)

Scripture tells us it is possible for our Lord of Peace to give us His peace at all times and in every situation.[61] So I follow God's instructions to let the peace of God guide my heart. I'm progressing in my growth to check with His Word to test every voice I hear, every leading I get and every decision I make. The more time we spend studying and meditating on the Word and the more time we spend in God's Presence worshiping and fellowshipping with Him, the more familiar we become with distinguishing His Voice from the enemy's voice or our own thoughts. Then peace prevails when we are confident of His leading.

The Lord tells us to, *"Be still, and know that I am God!..."*[62] He wouldn't have told us to do something we couldn't do! I've learned it is not only possible to do, but also very important to get quiet before God in an attitude of worship. Then I can hear Him speak to my heart and guide me so I can follow His will for me and avoid the enemy's traps. I'm steadily becoming more intentional to check for His peace in my heart and to allow it to be the ruling factor to confirm or reject any leading or my own decision. His affirming peace gives me great assurance that I'm hearing God correctly and I'm on the right path in His will.[63]

STAY ALERT

> *Stay alert! Watch out for your great enemy, the devil. He prowls around like a roaring lion, looking for someone to devour.* (1 Peter 5:8 NLT)

I grew up weighted with tormenting thoughts that kept me in a place of hopelessness and depression. It was my normal. At the time, I didn't know that many of those thoughts of rejection, self-abasement, fear and hopelessness did not originate from me, but they were pushed on me by evil spirits. Sadly, it didn't get much better as I grew into adulthood, for my thoughts were still almost completely negative and self-defeating.

After my salvation, I continued to struggle with oppressive thoughts and feelings until I learned enough of the Word of God and grew strong enough to resist the things that pulled me low. Over time, I gained more understanding, strength and wisdom from God to immediately recognize my enemy in many situations. Then the Lord exhorted me to be on the alert and immediately resist the smallest inkling of a downhearted oppression of any kind, including discouragement and frustration. He also alerted my heart to resist any feeling of fear at the onset. *Don't give it a moment's attention and keep in mind it is ALWAYS from the enemy.*

I now see these thoughts and feelings as fiery darts from the enemy that I must resist with my shield of faith (which is the Word of God) that I believe and speak as my personal confession.[64]

Therefore, I read the Word daily to grow my faith and keep it strong, and I speak daily confessions that give answers in the areas of my needs, weaknesses, and concerns. The foundation for my overcoming life and my peace is built on these daily routines.

Furthermore, I follow God's instructions to receive the peace that Jesus has given to His own. That is, I resist worry, and instead pray about all my needs and concerns while thanking God in everything. With His help, I also cast down all thoughts except for those that are true, honest, right, pure, lovely and of a good report. As long as I do this, His peace keeps my mind and heart free just as He said it would.[65]

Before I got to this place of stability in my life, I first learned the hard way that once a victory is won and things are going well with no threatening storms on the horizon, not to drop faith and just drift along in life until another big problem blindsides me. I learned to keep growing my faith when things are good, especially in my areas of weakness. I got this wisdom from the Lord when I became fed up with living a yo-yo life of pressing into God to get delivered from a problem, relaxing with the victory, then getting hit hard again and repeating the scenario with another problem that I was not prepared to deal with.

One day, in an exasperated state of mind, I told the Lord that I was tired of living that way. He spoke to my heart that if I would press in as much in the good times as I did in the bad, I would never have another down day. In other words, if I would not wait for a crisis to get serious about my time with God and His Word, I would be prepared to easily handle situations and not allow them to pull me down. That word from Him is what sparked the start of my daily routines of

"In the midst of a crisis, it doesn't matter how intense or serious the situation appears to be, stay calm and focused on Me and you'll always hear My answer."

spending time with Him and steadily confessing His Word over my life in order to stop giving the devil open places to attack me.[66] I still have to deal with problems arising periodically, but they no longer pull me down and stop my progress. Even in crisis situations, I am now able to do what the Lord instructed on March 22, 2022:

> *"In the midst of a crisis, it doesn't matter how intense or serious the situation appears to be, stay calm and focused on Me and you'll always hear My answer."*

Hiding His Word in my heart gives me all the strong faith I need to keep my eyes on Him and off problems–not only personal problems but also the problems of the world.

2

KEEP A WATCH OVER THE MOUTH

...if you've thought about saying something
stupid, you'd better shut your mouth.
Proverbs 30:32 TPT

"You'll be better off if you don't talk so much," the Lord said to me many years ago while fellowshipping with a group of prayer people who, along with myself, were excessively sharing with each other instead of praying according to our plan. That warning caused me to recall the Scripture:

In the multitude of words sin is not lacking, but he
who restrains his lips is wise. (Proverbs 10:19 NKJV)

Since then, I have been progressively getting better at being slow to speak and better at listening without trying to make too much small talk and unnecessary comments. This new attitude helps me stay free from violating the commandment to love one another, by not judging, gossiping and negatively critiquing when it's not my business to do so. At the same time, I am now carefully choosing what I say so that I can be wise and not in any way be snared by words that would cause harm to myself or others.[67]

I found out years ago that restraining my lips from speaking out of my feelings and emotions is not only vital to my love walk but it also plays a vital part in my liberation from bondages that once held me captive. I understand well the strength of sin that can flow from an emotion-driven, uncontrolled mouth because that was the way I used to react whenever I reached my climax of anger or stress. With each incident, I ended up spewing poison on a relationship and feeling more hopelessly trapped in a low place that I didn't want to be in.

I thank God for opening my eyes to the Truth that putting the Word in my heart helps me renew my mind so I can control my mouth and let Him be in control of my life. What a difference this has made in my relationships–not only with others, but also with God.

putting the Word in my heart helps me renew my mind so I can control my mouth

Jesus let me know that my words can get me into trouble when I read what He told the Pharisees:

> You can be sure of this: when the day of judgment comes, everyone will be held accountable for every careless word he has spoken. Your very words will be used as evidence against you, and your words will declare you either innocent or guilty." (Matthew 12:36-37 TPT)

That Scripture put the fear of God in me and played a part to help me control my mouth and filter my words. Adding to that, the revelation that I will have what I say, good or bad, inspired me even more to shut my mouth unless I truly have something good to say that lines up with God's Word and what I want.[68]

Emma Beacham

OPEN YOUR MOUTH

I am the Lord your God...Open your mouth wide, and I will fill it. (Psalm 81:10 NKJV)

Years ago, while believing God for an answer, I found myself sitting in a stupor, allowing doubt to swirl around my head and capture my thoughts. Thankfully, the Lord gave me a good wake-up call when He graciously said in a rebuking tone, *"Open your mouth!"* Then I got busy doing what He said to do and started resisting the doubt by speaking the Word of God on which I was basing my faith. As always, doubt fled, and I eventually received my answer.[69]

I had learned early in my Christian life that our faith must speak what we believe or it's not true faith.[70] Even so, at times I still found myself speaking negatively or not speaking the Word consistently enough to affirm my faith and/or counter doubt and fear that came to my mind. I worked hard on renewing my mind to the utter importance of the power of my words and how they affect every aspect of my life. My faith is much stronger now, and I'm more alert to speak God's Word than ever before; however, at times I still need a wake-up call from my Helper.

In January 2022, I needed to be alerted to my need to release my faith when the Lord said to me, *"Let your mouth lead the way."* He said that because again He had to remind me to open my mouth to agree with His Word and decree what I'm believing for. I've learned He wants us to participate in receiving the answers to prayer. I have also learned through experience that speaking the Word is especially needed for me to get the victory when resisting the works of the enemy that I often deal with. With God's help, I keep watch over my mouth to know when to shut it and when to open it and speak the Truth that brings freedom.

"Let your mouth lead the way."

42

CONSEQUENCES

The Lord once said to me, *"Don't let your mouth give satan something to work with against you."*

Even though I have learned the value of our words, and how they can give place to God to bless or to the enemy to curse, at times I have still messed up and caused myself trouble.

The first time I got pneumonia in February 2010, I didn't know how I contracted it or what had caused it to come upon me so suddenly. I was in the play area at church watching over the 4- and 5-year-olds as they ran around and played, and I started feeling chilled to the bone. Everything rapidly went downhill from there until I was extremely fatigued and struggling to breathe through inflamed lungs. As I prayed, the Lord diagnosed me with double pneumonia. I proceeded to receive my healing with the application of Scriptures declaring Jesus' sacrifice that paid the price for our health and wholeness.[71] It was tough going at times and took about a month, but the healing came.

Eleven years later, in August 2021, my sister and I went to a Christian conference in Fort Worth, Texas. As usual, the auditorium was cold, especially towards the end of the week. Adding to that, the thermostat in our hotel room didn't work properly. Even though we were well prepared with sweaters and fleece shawls, we were uncomfortable and started 'discussing' how cold it was in the building and in our room. Of course, we were cautious not to outright complain because we knew that was wrong, but we kept 'discussing' it.

When the conference ended, I went home to Tulsa, and she went back to Atlanta. Very shortly, I began getting sicker and sicker until I was extremely fatigued with no appetite and dangerously labored breathing. All the while I claimed my healing with no physical improvement. It appeared that I had contracted pneumonia again, only this time, instead of double it felt like triple! (Although I know I only have two lungs!)

After a few days of getting worse and not better, I felt I needed agreement in prayer, so I called my sister for help. To my surprise, she had gone to the doctor and been diagnosed with pneumonia. When I told her I had it too, we both agreed on how we got it– our big mouths 'discussing' how cold it was opened the door to the enemy. We knew better. In fact, we'd known better for many years.[72] The very conference we were attending was teaching us the importance of only speaking faith-filled words which God can use to bless us and not to speak negative words that our enemy can use against us. Yet, somehow we allowed ourselves to get duped by the devil and he did use our own words against us.

I got another prayer partner to pray and agree with me for my healing while I kept healing Scriptures and teachings ongoing daily. Around the tenth day, I was back to normal, except for the excessive phlegm that lingered for months.

In the light of that blunder and the humongous negative consequences, I have increased my watchfulness over my words by asking the Lord for His consistent assistance. That is, I have since added new Scriptures to my daily confession of His Word– Scriptures that request His help in watching my words, and if necessary, to interrupt me at any time I need to be put in check.[73] I choose to only speak what I want and not to say anything that I see, hear, think or feel which would cause me to curse myself.

OUR TESTIMONY OF FAITH AND VICTORY

> *And they overcame him by the Blood of the Lamb and by the Word of their testimony, and they did not love their lives to the death.* (Revelation 12:11 NKJV)

The Lord pointed out to me that the Scripture above did not say they overcame satan by prayer. Instead, they overcome him by their testimony about what the Blood of Jesus has done for them; and likewise, we overcome him and all his works by our personal testimony about what the Blood has bought and paid for. Obviously, it is the Word of God that we believe, speak, and live out that makes it our own testimony.[74]

Jesus Himself is our example of how to use the Word of God to defeat satan's temptations when He was in the wilderness.[75] He boldly spoke the Word as the answer, and we must do the same. I'm very grateful that I learned shortly after I was saved that satan is defeated by Jesus, not just in the wilderness, but most importantly on the Cross and in His Resurrection. Also, through His great victory won for us, He made us more than conquerors. So our responsibility is to simply enforce His victory with the authority that He delegated to us, by believing and speaking it.[76] This is the revelation that delivered me from the victim mentality, and gave me the mindset of a victor.

This is the revelation that delivered me from the victim mentality, and gave me the mindset of a victor.

SPEAK THE WORD FAITHFULLY

> *...he who has My word, let him speak My word faithfully...Is not My word like fire...? says the Lord, and like a hammer that breaks in pieces the rock [of most stubborn resistance]? (Jeremiah 23:28-29 AMPC)*

The Lord said to me on September 9, 2011:

> *"Hold the Word high with extreme confidence concerning what you know I have led you to do and accomplish. The stronger your resolve to know your God's faithfulness and love to keep you, provide*

45

> *for you, and exalt you, the weaker you make your*
> *enemy to hold out against you, and he must flee."*[77]

Therefore, I liken the consistent speaking (confessing) the Word to be like a spiritual hammer that is breaking (resisting) the enemy's work every time it is spoken with faith.

The Bible tells us to stand strong against the devil with the weapons of warfare the Lord has given us to overcome him. It tells us these weapons are mighty through God to destroy strongholds. One of our weapons is called the Sword of the Spirit which is the Word of God–or utterance of God's Word. Our declaration of the Word not only hammers but also cuts into the spirit realm and causes the enemy to flee.[78]

My daughter and I put this into practice when we consistently confessed out loud a particular Word that God gave us to get an unjust ticket dropped.[79]

After I was saved, I still had weaknesses of low self-esteem, self-condemnation, anger, fear, and bouts of depression from which I needed deliverance in order to be completely free from satan's traps that kept ensnaring me. Studying, meditating and consistently confessing specific Scriptures that deliberately addressed those weak areas broke the strength of these deeply entrenched bondages and washed them out of me over time.[80] However, I can't count the number of times that I considered giving up because it wasn't easy. In my heart, however, I knew if those weaknesses were left untouched, satan would inevitably use them against me to disrupt, defeat, and if possible, destroy my life and family.[81]

On another note, I have learned the hard way that once a victory is won and/or when things are going well with no threatening storms on the horizon, it is not wise to drop my faith and drift along in life. Otherwise, when the next storm came, my faith would be weak, and the problem would get the best of me before I could get victory over it. Instead, I learned to stay strong by depending on the Lord's strength while daily fellowshipping with the Holy Spirit and spending time in the Word and in His Presence.[82]

As I was learning how to conquer the many problems and challenges I often faced, the Lord spoke to me in December 2006:

> *"Let the Word of God you're standing on fight the battle. Your tongue swings the sword of God's promised Word to cut away all that opposes. Don't speak what you see, but speak what you seek.*

We also overcome satan by speaking the Word of God as our personal testimony whenever we are tempted or attacked with a problem.[83] We are instructed that we must confess God's Word to receive all our Redemption rights and benefits that Jesus paid the price to give us.[84] Romans 10:10 says that with our mouths we confess to receive salvation, which includes healing, safety and preservation. Therefore, after confessing and receiving Jesus as my Lord and Savior, I learned to also confess my deliverance from an invasion of sickness, disease, and every work of the devil.[85] I also confess safety Scriptures–such as Psalm 91–to receive our Covenant protection from danger, including plagues, diseases and attacks of the enemy.

Don't speak what you see, but speak what you seek.

In the early years of my Christian life, I didn't know much about taking authority over the devil, but I had learned much about the power and authority in God's Word when we speak it with faith. Confessing the Word is how I received most of my victories over the devil when he tried to revisit me with past bondages. For instance, my relationship with my

Confessing the Word is how I received most of my victories over the devil when he tried to revisit me with past bondages.

husband became very strained after several years of marriage, and some of my former bondages tried to entangle me again. I once dealt with a lot of anger and hate where at times I would erupt in an uncontrollable rage. However, by then I had determined to allow God's love to rule my life.

One day after we argued, I went to my bedroom, upset and hurting, when suddenly an almost overwhelming feeling of hate tried to come upon me. Immediately, I cried out the Word from my heart: "I can't hate, because the LOVE OF GOD is shed abroad in my heart by the Holy Ghost!"[86] I actually surprised myself with my strong response because it flowed out of me so radically. I kept repeating that Word for a few minutes until the feeling of hate left me. In contemplating why I blurted out, "I can't hate," it came to me that it's impossible to hate someone while releasing the love of God to them.[87] Even while I was struggling with my emotions, my decision to love directed my heart's response and caused my enemy to be defeated. This happened a few more times until my inner self was strengthened by the Word and personal time with the Lord to the point that the enemy could no longer successfully use the strongholds of offense and strife against me.[88]

I did a similar thing after another argument with my husband that left me feeling so worthless that a spirit of insanity (like the one I had encountered when I was in the psychiatric ward of the hospital) came upon me as if a bird had landed on my head. It came upon me so strongly that I shouted, "God has not given me a spirit of fear, but of power, love and a SOUND MIND!"[89] I kept confessing that Scripture until the spirit left me.

I'm grateful that I learned early in my Christian life that true faith believes and speaks–so I speak what I believe.[90] Believing and speaking the Word keeps me in agreement with God. It keeps me speaking the power of God into my situation by confessing the Word of His power.[91]

true faith believes and speaks–so I speak what I believe.

Many years ago, I was in a season where I was experiencing a lot of lack and was struggling with my faith. During that time, my confessions of God's Word were dry and lifeless. The Lord alerted me to my lack of faith and gave me the phrase, *"praise confessions."* He was reminding me to speak His Word with joy and expectancy. Confessions spoken in faith activate the power of praise ensuring the enemy's defeat. As a result, the answers I need will manifest![92]

Time and time again, I am led by the Lord to confess certain Scriptures over my body, and I have been healed of everything from small pains to major illnesses. Better yet, there was a time when He helped me avoid sickness by leading me to confess healing Scriptures over myself beforehand.

At the end of 1997, I was feeling just fine when, for no apparent reason, the Lord instructed me to go to a Christian bookstore and get a small book on healing confessions to speak over myself. I said, "Yes Sir," and proceeded to procrastinate for several more weeks when He again reminded me to get it. Again, I affirmed with good intentions to get it soon. Instead, I kept procrastinating until He firmly warned me one day that He was trying to protect me from an attack of sickness so get the book and confess the Scriptures!

Then I knew it was serious! I hurried and chose one that I felt was the best for me. The Lord instructed me to confess the Scriptures twice daily. On January 1, 1998, I started and kept at it for 2½ months until one morning the Lord spoke to my heart, *"That which was planted is dissolved and rooted out of your body."* What was dissolved? I have no idea, and I don't care to know. I do know the enemy's assignment against me was thwarted so it couldn't take me down or even kill me.

I once heard a minister say to build your arsenal of Truth. Since the Word is Truth,[93] that is what the book of healing Scriptures gave me. I got an arsenal of Truth to use as weapons against the enemy of sickness that was attempting to carry out an attack against me before I even knew it. God knew and graciously helped me to avoid something terrible. I am very grateful for the warning and for His patience with me.

BRAG ON THE GREATER ONE

...our boast is in the Lord our God, who makes us strong and gives us victory! (Psalm 20:7 TPT)

In my quest to put God first and live by faith, I have learned that we should never talk about the big and scary things the devil is doing or going to do against us as if he's a match for God. Instead, we should always keep in mind and confidently acknowledge God's power which is so much greater than the enemy's opposition. To be victorious, we declare what the Lord God is doing and will do for us that absolutely trumps all the activities of the kingdom of darkness.

After I moved to Tulsa and started in the prayer ministry in October 2000, I considered myself a novice compared to some of the other prayer people with whom I worked. So I observed carefully when we had group prayer so I could learn as I participated. One disturbing thing I noticed was the lopsided attention often given to the strength of the enemy to harm versus the strength of God to help. Many times, the devil seemed to get more respect. I found I had to be careful not to become too devil conscious myself after times of hearing too much talk about him. I knew that couldn't have been the attitude the Lord meant for us to take regarding our enemy when He told us to be watchful of him.

To have an attitude of a victor, I receive God's Word as personally speaking to me:

The more I grow in the knowledge of the Lord, the more I understand how vital it is for me to fix my mind on Jesus–by fixing my mind on the Word which has all the answers. This enables me to stay calm and know that my victory is inevitable in His triumph. To have an attitude of a victor, I receive God's Word as personally speaking to me:

> *Little children (believers, dear ones), you are of God and you belong to Him and have [already] overcome them [the agents of the antichrist]; because He who is in you is greater than he (Satan) who is in the world [of sinful mankind].* (1 John 4:4 AMP)

There is no competition! The Greater One is in me and for me! The devil is already defeated by our Champion, Jesus! And because He won, we can also win every time![94]

I am also reminded of the experience my four-year-old son had when he was being tormented by evil spirits. As he put it, whenever the devil and his demons came to harass him, he would call on Jesus, who would come with His angels and whip the devil and his gang. Consequently, Jesus delivered him from satan's harassment.[95]

Proverbs 3:6 encourages us to acknowledge God in everything, and He will direct our path. That became my goal in life–to put my Lord at the center of all I do and include Him in everything. I find this to be the best way to be alert and keep watch against the workings of the devil. When I give Him the glory and declare His Word in a situation, He is faithful to see that what He has promised will come to pass.[96]

3

WATCH OVER THE CHILDREN

Then the people brought their little children to Jesus so that he could lay his hands on them to bless them and pray for them. When the followers saw this, they told the people to stop bringing their children to him. But Jesus said, "Let the little children come to me. Don't stop them, because God's kingdom belongs to people who are like these children."
Matthew 19:13-14 ERV

Over the years, I have had the privilege of working with many children. I led a youth group and choir in the small Baptist Church we attended in Florida. For three years, my children and I also had a Kid's Club Ministry with the neighborhood kids in our apartment complex in East Tulsa. In addition, I volunteered and worked with children in our church's Bus Ministry and our Inner-City Youth Ministry in Tulsa. I was also employed with our church Children's Ministry for five years, and I have been volunteering with our Tulsa Dream Center Kid's Ministry for over ten years.

So I have had a lot of interactions and relationships with many children over the decades. There's at least one thing they all have in common: they all need the guidance and protection of mature adults. Even more so, they need spiritual guidance and protection to deliver them from natural troubles and most importantly from satan and his many demonic cohorts who are always looking for ways to steal, kill and destroy them.[97] They need those who have obtained the knowledge of the Truth of God's Word to watch over them with love and prayer.[98]

When my children were young, the Lord started telling me to keep watch over them at certain times. I was led to get alone with Him and present them to Him one by one. I would write down what He gave me for each one, pray it through, and speak to them about it if necessary. During these times, I was informed of things I needed to know and instructed on how to handle them. I was also warned of some of satan's plans and given wisdom to thwart those plans. That doesn't mean that I knew everything or that I was aware of everything my children were going through. We still had struggles and problems to deal with, and we still had needs. However, by consistently covering them in prayer and speaking the Word over them, I became more sensitive to many things that were going on in their lives that would have negatively altered their destinies. So in positioning myself to hear from God by setting aside time to seek the Lord on behalf of my children, I was greatly helped in raising them and in protecting them from the devil and his tactics.

Praying and blessing my children at bedtime helped me guide them away from the snares of the devil and deal correctly with the encounters of life. The Lord gave me a specific blessing that was designed for them and instructed me to declare it nightly over each one individually as I laid my hand on them. It took time, but it was my pleasure to present them to God so He could bless them and help them fulfill their destinies.

(I believe it is best to get specifics from the Lord on what to pray and how to bless the child, for only He knows what they need going forward. Because our God sees what we can't see, and knows what we don't know, including the future, He can thwart satan's works against them before the enemy can carry out his evil schemes against them.)[99]

As I have grown in my own walk with the Lord, I have learned how to keep watch over my grandchildren even better than I did my children. By the time my third grandchild came along, I had improved my watching. While they were still in the womb, I started praying and confessing the Word of God over them daily to bless them and to counter potential problems that would more than likely be handed down from the issues their parents had or still struggled with. As they grow and display tendencies, attitudes and bents that need to be tweaked or changed by the grace of God, I add my faith and confessions to support their parents. I claim the promises given to me to bless my offspring.[100]

I also take every opportunity to teach and discipline them to help them choose God's way and steer away from troubles that, by the Word and by experience, I know will come if the enemy is not discerned and resisted.

SPIRITUAL HERITAGE

I learned through the Word of God, through teachings from others and through personal experience that children will more than likely face the same sins, struggles and temptations that their parents faced or still face in their lives. Besides being trained to act like the parents, I believe many problems repeat into the next generation because the same spirits will look for ways to harass the children the way they harassed the parents.[101]

Over the years, I heard teachings that called these passed-down problems 'generational curses.' Jesus redeemed us from the curse, but the enemy will still try to carry out the curse on our children if we don't resist him and make him flee.[102] Therefore, after many years of gaining understanding, I believe it's more appropriate to call them 'generational demons.' I believe that better explains why the thing(s) some people hate the most about their parents (and often swear they would never do), they end up being driven to do the same.

Therefore, I endeavor to watch out for evil spirits that intimidate, terrify and attack the children. I don't know why the little ones tend to remain silent when tormented, but they most often do. I remained silent when I was tormented as a child. By the grace of God, I learned to pay attention to my children (sometimes with a nudge from God) to notice unusual reactions and behavior, and then get insight from the Lord on how to deal with the situations.

The Good News is that the demonic assignments against the family can be canceled and the harassments stopped. I know they can because I've experienced it in my life and family.

Generational Fear

In 1993, my sister and I attended a Christian conference together in Fort Worth, Texas. She flew from Chicago, and my four children and I drove from Sanford, Florida. Since they did not have services for small children, my two youngest, ages two and four years old, attended the services with us. We attended every service in the week-long meeting except one. With three services a day, by Saturday night they were both exhausted and slept through the entire last service. The minister taught on getting delivered from fear. Then he gave a command for fear to leave everyone present.

I had been working with my four-year-old for a long time to help him with overwhelming fear that would suddenly come upon him. At times he would be too terrified to go back to his room in the middle of the night. Early on, he would tell me he saw monsters before he realized they were actually demons. At times when he told me he saw something, I would take him back to his room and look around with him to prove there was nothing there. I didn't know any better at that time.

On the way to the car, he looked up at me and gleefully proclaimed, "Mommy, I ain't scared of the devil no more!" To our surprise and amazement, he started telling us about experiences starting when he was around three years old of the devil and his demons appearing to him and tormenting him with fear.

He went on to share what he had been going through for the past year and a half. After suffering with the fear that the enemy brought with his visitations, he said one night an angel came and told him to call for Jesus whenever the devil came. He began to do just that. He told many stories of Jesus and his angels coming to help him when the devil and his demons showed up. It was fascinating, and we believed every word because his heart was so pure. His stories caused some past things he had done to finally make sense—things where I did not understand why he acted the confusing way he did at times. His experiences with the demons appearing to him explained everything.

He was asleep during the service when the command releasing him from fear had been given at the service, so he didn't know what had happened. He just knew what he kept repeating, "I ain't scared of the devil no more!"

When we got to the hotel room, I put everyone to bed, and they all went to sleep except my four-year-old, who was too hyped to sleep. After I finished my shower, he was even more hyped as he told me what had happened while I was out of the room. An angel came again, he said, and told him something about inviting Jesus into his heart, and he did. (Apparently, he was reminded of what he had been taught about salvation.) Then he said the devil came back and told him that he wouldn't bother him again as long as he didn't call Jesus anymore. This four-year-old was smarter than that, so he called on Jesus again. This time Jesus came and grabbed the devil. Then He opened the door to the room, threw the devil out, and closed the door. That was the last time he had those demonic visitations.

Was it actually the devil that appeared to that four-year-old?

Good question. All I know is that he had frequent visitations from evil spirits, whom he called the devil and his demons. Regardless of which evil spirits they were, Jesus took care of them for my little boy.

Furthermore, the Lord saw to it that I got enough information to understand that those visitations from satan to terrorize him were not assigned to him only, but they were actually generational. At different times, his father and grandfather shared with me their similar experiences with visitations from evil spirits. His father was terrorized by evil spirits appearing to him in the form of dead loved ones from the time he was a child into his adulthood. They terrorized his grandfather in the form of ghosts (or 'hants' as he called them) appearing to him. I believe it stops with my son.

Generational Rejection

My husband wanted a lot of children, and it suited him well that the first three looked more like him than me. However, when my fourth child was born, she didn't look like my husband, but she looked very much like me. Elated for the fourth time, I was mesmerized by my beautiful baby and very thankful that I had her in my life. Unfortunately, my husband didn't share my enthusiasm about his fourth child.

When our first child was born, he told me, "That's not my baby." I thought he was serious, and it hurt deeply for him to deny his child. It was his way of joking to get a reaction out of me, and react I did. When I had our second child, he said the same thing, "That's not my baby." It angered me again for him to say that, but I realized by the smirk that accompanied the comment, it was just another joke to jab at me. Again, when our third child was born, with a bigger smirk he said the same thing, even as he gloated over his son. Wisely, that time I gave no attention to his antics. In light of the three previous experiences, I wasn't surprised to hear the same phrase for the fourth time. Only this time it was said differently. He said it with a heart-piercing, disdaining tone that made it clear that he really meant it.

The last baby didn't quite fit his pattern. I knew that he knew I didn't cheat on him, but that didn't seem to matter. I even asked him if he believed I cheated. When he tried to avoid the question, I pushed for an answer until he hesitantly said no. However, he still wouldn't accept the baby. He even repeated again, "That's not my baby." How irrational! (I often say that the devil is irrational so it's no surprise when those who yield to him are irrational.) He wouldn't touch her, and the way he looked at her reminded me of how my father used to look at me to create trembling fear in me. In fact, everything about the matter totally reminded me of my father's relationship with me.

When I was a child, I endured 12 years of my father's disdaining looks and attitude that no doubt was a big part of my many problems while growing up. Even at that young age, it was clear that he had a despising hatred for me as though I had done him wrong. Of course, I didn't know what I had done, and I wouldn't find out my violation until I was 26 years old and graduating from college.

At my graduation, my mother was so happy for me, and she exclaimed that she knew I would make it. Then she unwittingly disclosed that my father didn't think I was his child, and he didn't think I would amount to anything. She kept on talking to praise me, but I didn't take in anything else she said. Instead, my mind revisited my childhood encounters with my father, and I silently spoke to myself, "So that's why he hates me."

I also recalled in my memories how jealous my father was of my mother, and how I look very much like her. I then realized that my violation against my father was that I looked too much like my mother and not enough like him. I also believe that Momma added insult to injury when she named me after his mother.

Thirty-six years after my father rejected me for the way I looked, I was witnessing my husband doing the very same thing for the very same reason to our daughter. I knew I could not stand by and allow her to suffer the same consequences that I had suffered through the years. By that time in my Christian walk, I recognized the trademark plan of the devil to try and destroy her like he almost destroyed me. Even so, I still hoped that her daddy would drop the foolishness and bond with his daughter.

It took several weeks for me to realize that he did not intend to change his attitude. At that point, hurting and weeping, I sat down in my rocking chair and talked to my Lord. Cuddling my baby girl while rocking back and forth, I told the Lord that as much as I wanted to obey Him, I could not stand by and allow this child to suffer like I did. My own conscience wouldn't allow it. If he doesn't accept her, I reasoned with the Lord, I need to leave him for her sake. I believed that He would either turn my husband's heart towards his daughter or release me from the marriage.

Although my husband was very susceptible to the lies and deceptions of the devil, our Lord knew how to turn his heart the right way when the situation required it, and I got to watch it happen! Within days, he totally changed his attitude towards the baby. He not only began to hold her, but he also helped feed and even change her diaper! In fact, he started doing more for her than he did for any of our other children. He cuddled her frequently and didn't want to put her down. Before, he would not keep the children while I went to the store, but after falling in love with his new baby, he volunteered to keep her and the other three. It was joyfully amazing to observe!

Even with that great victory, the enemy tried to repeat the curse into the next generation when my baby girl grew up and got pregnant out of wedlock. The father didn't believe the baby was his. So there was no communication for two and a half years until something clicked that caused him to want to meet his child. The end result is they came together as a family and got married about a year and a half later. Of course, there was much prayer and declaration for that baby to have a good loving father–and she now has one. Thank God for His amazing grace!

Any curse perpetuated by satan can and should be broken with the Word of God that addresses the situation and with the Blood of Jesus that redeems us from every work of the enemy!

WATCH FOR IRRITATIONS AND CHANGE IN CHARACTER

When my son was seven years old, he went through an experience where he was downcast and constantly sad for weeks. He was often very irritable and touchy, which was unlike him. When I confronted him with certain issues, he cried very easily, and he never knew why. When I took time to seek the Lord for answers, He informed me that it was due to a 'spirit of oppression.'[103] So I cast it off him, and immediately he said he felt better. We praised God for His goodness!

The ordeal made me realize that a young child being raised by a struggling single mother and her sister presents weaknesses that the enemy can exploit, but the Good News for us is that, by the grace of God, all of his evil works can be undone.[104]

WATCH OUT FOR IRRATIONAL FEAR

We also had several occasions when my children and grandchildren experienced incidences of extreme fear that proved to be nothing but satanic attacks against them. Over the years, when they were very young, more than one of them would go from being fearless to being suddenly terrified to enter a certain area of the house, such as when my son experienced the demonic visitations from the generational demons of fear. Other experiences included more than one of my grandchildren suddenly becoming too afraid to go down the hallway to the bathroom of my daughter's home until we evicted the spirit frightening them.

When my oldest granddaughter was about four years old, she suddenly became too afraid to walk down my sidewalk. Since she was a fearless little girl, it was surprising when she started stopping a few feet from my front door and refusing to go past a certain point. From then on, her mother would have to practically drag her along or pick her up and carry her to and from my house. Then I noticed how she was visibly afraid of something she appeared to be seeing.

Although I never sensed any demonic presence in that area, I have come to recognize some of the signs of the enemy's effect on children. So one day I went to the spot where she always stalled, and I addressed the enemy and commanded him to leave my property in Jesus' Name.[105] After that, she had no more problems walking on my sidewalk.

I did a similar thing with two other grandchildren when they went from being fearless to suddenly being too afraid to go down the hall to the bathroom. After several times of observing their terrified reaction when they reached a certain point, I realized they were seeing or sensing something we couldn't see. So one day I took authority over the spirit of fear in that hallway, and the children were free to go down it without being forced.

In 2009, I started working in the children's ministry for our Sunday morning and Wednesday night church services. For five years, I worked with four- and five-year-olds. We received the children in our play zone, then we'd separate the age groups and take them to their classrooms after play time. When one sweet four-year-old turned five, she had an unusually difficult time advancing to the next group. In fact, she was absolutely too terrified to join them, so we allowed her to stay with the fours for a while longer.

One Sunday, her mother brought her at the end of playtime when we were separating the groups, but when she started leading her daughter to the five-year-old class, she resisted greatly with extreme fear. Her mother was frustrated and baffled because she was normally a very obedient child. After observing this, I began to pray for her to be freed from the fear that gripped her.

The next time I observed her mother dropping her off, the Lord allowed me to see in the spirit, and I saw a monkey-like demon hanging on the child's back. God led me to quietly take authority over it to free her, and I did. Well, I knew the result would speak for itself the next time she came to church, and it did! I was on the lookout for her, so when her mother brought her in, I watched intently as the child confidently joined the five-year-olds with no hesitation. Silently, I praised our Lord God for His great love and goodness to set every captive free!

WATCH FOR EXTREME EMOTIONAL PROBLEMS

While preparing to go to my mother's funeral in February 1985, a strong Spirit of prayer came upon me for my family. I ended up spending hours in prayer where I perceived the Lord was preparing me to talk to some family members about Him. I didn't know who; I just knew I needed to be ready to speak whatever He gave me to say at the moment.

Shortly after I arrived there, my eighteen-month-old daughter started acting very strangely. She began constantly whining and clinging to me. Soon I had to carry her in my arms everywhere I went while she whined and cried the whole time as if she was in distress. That, of course, made it very difficult to talk to anyone. By just observing, I'm certain she appeared to be a very spoiled child, which she was not. However, something was wrong, but I had no clue what it was. Finally, when I looked in her eyes and I saw torment, I got serious and sought the Lord for an answer. *"It's a spirit,"* the Lord revealed. Then He told me to get it off her! I commanded it to leave her, and immediately she began to get better. Soon she returned to herself.

I almost wanted to kick myself for not recognizing the enemy sooner. Instead, I allowed the devil to torment my child and almost interrupt God's plans. I believe I was hindered from discerning the enemy because I was frustrated with my daughter. Therefore, I closed God out of the situation, until I looked in her eyes and realized she was being tormented. Then the compassion of God rose up in me towards her, and my love connected with Love Himself, putting me in a position to hear Him speak the answer for her deliverance. (Eventually, I learned that to communicate and receive from God, we have to be on the same frequency as Him–the Love frequency!)

The Good News is, besides it being a good learning experience, I shared the Gospel with three of my sisters and led them to give their lives to the Lord. The greatest victory was when He rescued one of them from joining a cult which was at the point of reeling her into their group. I was able to present the true Gospel to her and uncover the false doctrine they were masking under the guise of Christianity.

The Lord had actually led me to prepare to minister His Truth to my sister weeks before the funeral when I felt compelled to do research on that same cult. Since their messengers often came to my home to recruit me, I had bought a pamphlet that outlined the differences between the cult and Christianity so I could prepare myself to minister to their recruiters. Little did I know that I would use that information to help my own sister.

In the light of the blessing of my three sisters accepting the Lord, it is no wonder the enemy tried so hard to distract and hinder me from communicating with my family.

WATCH FOR EXTREME ANGER

Our seven-year-old relative, who was usually a happy child, started having anger issues. He hurt some children at school and attempted to hurt my children when they were together. When I asked him why he was so angry, he said he didn't know. I then told him to give me a smile, and he couldn't do it. After many days of him being angry and hateful towards almost everyone, I sought the Lord for an answer.

The Lord revealed to me that he had a 'spirit of anger' oppressing him. I asked him if he wanted to be free from it, and he said yes. I commanded the evil spirit to go from him. The tense, angry look left his face, and he could smile again. He had been set free.

4

WATCH OUT FOR ENTERTAINMENT

Do not be so deceived and misled! Evil companionships
(communion, associations) corrupt and deprave
good manners and morals and character.
1 Corinthians 15:33 AMPC

The Lord said to me in July 2009, *"Your body is going to want what you feed your mind."* It's easy to see that advertisers understand this truth, so they bombard us with images of food, new styles of clothing, etc.

> *"Your body is going to want what you feed your mind."*

However, I believe the Lord was especially alluding to those things to which we open our minds while engaging in ungodly literature and sinfully enticing visual entertainment and music (especially sexually charged music and images).

It's common knowledge that emotions and urges are stirred up through that which we watch, read, and hear. This is especially true in the areas of fear, hate and sex. Unbeknown to most of us, demon spirits are free to entice and drive the emotions and urges while feeding our minds with that kind of entertainment. They often stick around and continue to drive those urges when the music stops, the book is finished, or the show is over. They are always looking for every opportunity to destroy lives, relationships and families in every way they can.[106] Therefore, I made it my purpose to train my children to choose the right entertainment and avoid the wrong.

ENTERTAINMENT THAT OPENS DOORS TO THE ENEMY

Movies and TV

One Sunday my daughter came home from Children's Church very impacted by the message. The teacher illustrated to them what happens in the spirit realm when they watch certain types of ungodly programming on TV. They had snakes crawling out of the mock TV, depicting demons being released into the atmosphere.[107] Then those demons are free to attack because they have been invited into the home. I was grateful for the support to help me explain why I was so selective about what I allowed them to watch.

A major reason why I was and am so cautious is because I had to deal with negative consequences from certain movies when the children were very young. I didn't approve and even protested when their daddy encouraged them to watch scary movies with him. Nightmares and monster sightings followed. Fear and more fear arrived, and I had to constantly comfort one tormented child. I tried to get my husband to understand the damage he was doing to the children by allowing and at times, even making them watch those frightening things, but he didn't get it. However, when we separated and I was fully in charge, I became very selective.

While most ungodly stuff is not that hard to spot, I learned we also have to be cautious about some seemingly harmless entertainment. Our enemy is crafty, and we all need God's wisdom and insight to avoid the enemy's deception.

When my children were in their early teens (one pre-teen), we moved into an apartment complex where they allowed the residents to check out free movies from the office. Because of our standards, the choices were limited. One day I chose a rather popular animation with a cute, devious main character. (I didn't know how devious it was at the time.) As I passed by the room where my children were watching it, I felt an alert in my heart to stop and observe for myself. While I watched, alarms went off within me, and I knew that a wrong spirit was involved in the making of that movie. That little character was more than just devious, he was demonic! I certainly didn't want to release a wrong spirit in my home. I was already beginning to have some slight problems with teenager disrespect and talking back, and I didn't want fuel added to the small fire already kindled. I made them stop the movie and take it back. They protested, reasoning that it was animated and the character, though devious, was cute and he would probably get better in the end. "Take it back!" I demanded, as the alarm in me increased to strengthen my stand! I tried to explain the wrong spirit in it, but I don't think they realized the gravity of it all.

My children were not very happy with me for taking away their supposedly, 'child-friendly' movie. I wasn't happy about it either, for their sake and for the fact that I now felt disconcerted about what movies to select, so I talked to the Lord about it. He answered by teaching me about moviemaking and all kinds of media. *"There are three types of entertainment,"* He said. Some entertainment is God-ordained, and His Spirit is on it. Some are neutral; it's just entertainment for fun/instruction/information. But some are from the domain of darkness with satan's agenda on it to steal, kill, and destroy.[108] He then warned me to check with Him and find out what kind of movie/entertainment it is before we open up to it.

Actually, we had already faced a similar experience with a four-year-old cousin several years earlier. He had a certain movie that he really liked. It was a modern remake of an old movie with cute, sassy kids misbehaving in very funny ways. In the old version, it worked well; however, the new version had a different feel to it. In particular, everytime our little cousin watched that movie he would start acting up and misbehaving as though he took on the naughty nature of the characters in the movie. We even did an experiment to make sure it was the effect of the movie, and sure enough it was.

I found a copy of the old version and we let him watch it. The children were hilariously just as naughty (or maybe even more so) as in the new movie. He enjoyed it, but it didn't affect him negatively. Then we let him rewatch the new version and the naughty nature showed up again. Needless to say, we got rid of the new and kept the old. In prayer, the Lord confirmed that an evil spirit was involved in the making of the new version, but not the old one.

During my many years of walking with the Lord and learning about the devices that satan uses to entrap and oppress us,[109] I have learned to immediately resist oppressive feelings at the onset from any source. That includes turning off entertainment when necessary to stop the spirit of heaviness, lust, fear, etc, from taking hold of me.[110] I worked with my children to teach them, and now we're working on teaching my grandchildren.

When my twelve-year-old grandson didn't want to eat or play games at my granddaughter's birthday party, I knew something had to be wrong. When I questioned him, he said he didn't feel good.

"Does your stomach hurt?"

"No," he replied.

"Where do you hurt?"

"I don't know; I just don't feel good," he answered. As I prayed for him, I discerned it was not physical, but spiritual. So I came against the spirit of oppression and heaviness, but I felt a hindrance to my prayer. Then I discerned the blockage was because of something he had watched.

With that understanding, I told him he needed to repent in order to give God the freedom to help him and to stop the work of the evil spirit he had given place to.[111] Then his mom and I taught him more on the importance of screening what he watches and listens to. In a little while, he was playing games with his friends.

Later I asked him if he knew what he had watched that opened the door to the enemy. He said yes; it was some scary movie. When I asked if he was going to be careful not to watch that kind of stuff anymore, he said yes. I went on to encourage him that he was blessed to understand now about how to stop and avoid opening the door because many people don't understand what makes them feel so bad at times. I told him that now he can help his friends by sharing his experience when they have similar problems and don't know why.

Music

When my children were very young, the Lord started talking to me about music. He said to me, *"Music is powerful."* He called my attention to the effects of Gospel music on our souls and the effects of ungodly music that stirs up unhealthy emotions and pollutes the mind. For a period of time, He kept repeating that phrase to me as I observed people enjoying certain music and singing lyrics to songs–good and bad. At first, I didn't take what He told me too seriously, but I soon realized He really wanted me to understand the importance of music to create atmosphere and influence lives. I came to understand that *"music is powerful!"*

Many years later when my thirteen-year-old became angry and rebellious, I discovered he had been listening to some horrible music that fed that kind of behavior. It was on a CD that a friend from his school had loaned him. It was truly the mercy of God that caused it to be revealed to me for his sake and for the sake of the family's peace and harmony. Upon exposure, I intended to crush the CD, but he begged me not to because he needed to return it. So I spared it but took measures to intervene in that relationship and cut off some other ungodly entertainment and wrong influences. In fact, I felt the need to pull him out of that school and homeschool him for a semester. Shortly, by cutting off the bad influences and reinforcing Kingdom of God principles, he was delivered, and I got my sweet child back.

Reading Materials

We have also experienced some negative consequences from reading the wrong material. When my twelve-year-old became sick and the Lord revealed to me that she had read the horoscope, it was obvious that an evil spirit had attacked her body through her reading that occultic material. When she repented, the enemy's work was thwarted, and she was healed.[112]

I thank our Lord for exposing the enemy every time and delivering us from his schemes and traps. As we watch and pray and put our trust in Him, He is truly faithful to undo every work of the devil against us and keep us free from evil.[113]

WHO IS FEEDING YOUR RELAXED MIND?

While watching a Star Wars movie, a commercial came on for a demented looking program series. After I muted and ignored it, the Lord spoke to my heart regarding it and other twisted and/ or evil TV programs to which I would not open my mind. In line with many thoughts I have had in the past about these kinds of programs and movies, He spoke:

> *"Think about who must be writing the scripts for these kinds of programs and movies. What kind of spiritual state must they be in to think up such things, and who do you think is driving their creative writings? With that in mind, who would want to allow such people to feed them their demonically driven imaginations? Yet many of My people,*

who have My Holy Spirit, regularly allow demon-inspired programming and movies to entertain them. Is it any wonder that so many of them are confused, faithless, trapped in bondages and have joined the world in accepting mental illness?"

5

WATCH YOUR THOUGHTS

*Above all, be careful what you think because
your thoughts control your life.*
Proverbs 4:23 ERV

Derek Prince, who taught extensively on demons, said, "Every voice is a personality." He was speaking of how demons feed thoughts into our minds. These voices that suggest and sometimes bombard our minds with thoughts meant to steal, kill and destroy in some way come from spirit personalities (evil spirits) that we can resist.

In my early childhood, I let my mind run wild all the time. I didn't filter my thoughts because I didn't know that I could. I practically stayed deep in thoughts that were mostly negative and full of self-pity. That's why I struggled with depression and thoughts of suicide for so many years, along with many other debilitating issues. Self-condemnation was a major problem that I rehearsed often, and it kept me in a very self-abased state of mind. As a result, I grew up being miserable all the time.

> *I didn't filter my thoughts because I didn't know that I could.*

Once saved, I learned that every thought that comes across

my mind does not necessarily originate from me, especially thoughts and feelings that oppress or try to pressure me to make wrong choices. Learning that the enemy is masterful at projecting his destructive plans into our minds has freed me from his control in many ways. I believe Judas betraying Jesus is a great example of how effective the devil can be in deceiving someone to carry out his devious plan. John 13:2 says the devil put the thought of betraying Jesus into the heart of Judas Iscariot. He didn't cast it down, so he became a betrayer. Likewise, whenever I would think wrong thoughts, I would speak wrong and do wrong. Now that I have planted God's thoughts in my heart, I am getting better at recognizing the wrong thoughts and rejecting them. So satan has lost the control over me that he once had. However, our enemy is very crafty and a great deceiver, so I know I must stay alert to quickly catch and reject thoughts and impressions from him. If it steals, kills and destroys, then he is the author.[114]

I've talked to more than one Christian who thought satan could read their minds because a negative thought would come to them and then it would happen. They assumed he read their mind and then carried out their unsavory thoughts. As far as I know, there's nothing Biblical to support that theory. However, over the years, I have found that the enemy is masterful at interjecting his thoughts and then observing our reactions to his suggestions. I've concluded that if the devil feeds someone a thought and it is not resisted, then he knows what the person is thinking. When the thought is accepted, he will act on what he planted. I have had more than one experience of that nature. The worst one taught me a lesson I'll never forget.

One late winter day, while working out in the gym, the thought came to me that I was going to pick up a virus and take it home with me. I usually rebuke those types of thoughts, but that day I had a 'duh' moment as I looked around the gym and thought, "Nobody looks sick in here." Then I kept working out.

In the next couple of days, I got sicker and sicker with the most miserable flu symptoms I have ever had. I prayed and confessed my healing Scriptures, rebuked the sickness, and took all the natural remedies that I had, but two weeks went by, and it didn't budge even a little bit. I had to constantly cover my nostrils because my right one felt like it was a wide open, endless tunnel that was drawing in and circulating frigid air throughout my whole system with every breath I took.

Finally, as I sought the Lord for answers to the root of the problem, He took me back in my mind to the gym when I made that foolish response to the thought that came to me that day. Then I saw that I had violated Scripture when I didn't reject the thought and resist the enemy.[115] My lack of resistance gave my enemy an open door to take advantage of me because I am responsible for using the knowledge I have acquired.[116] Upon seeing this error, the Lord strongly spoke to my heart, *"You brought it home with you!"* I knew He was referring to a spirit of infirmity[117] that I brought home from the gym that day. I permitted it to attach to me through my silent permission.

> *My lack of resistance gave my enemy an open door to take advantage of me because I am responsible for using the knowledge I have acquired.*

In the Name of Jesus, I commanded the evil spirit to leave my body, and thanked Jesus for delivering me. The symptoms began to subside right away until it was all gone in a few days.[118]

That experience reminded me that satan takes our silence to his proposals and threats as permission for him to carry them out. I learned the hard way never to ignore his threats thinking he'll just go away, but simply to rebuke his evil intentions and move on with my life untouched by him.

DON'T VIOLATE LOVE

> *If you keep My commandments, you will abide in My love, just as I have kept My Father's commandments and abide in His love...This is My commandment, that you love one another as I have loved you.* (John 15:10,12 NKJV)

The one commandment given to us in the New Testament is to love one another.[119] So it stands to reason that our enemy will do anything he can to get us to violate that directive from the Lord. Satan works to taint people's (especially leaders') images in our minds by sowing negative thoughts and pointing out faults–real or perceived. He wants us to judge and condemn one another. His goal is division because he knows that unity is power, but a house (family, group, church, Body of Christ, etc.) divided will fall.[120]

When my marriage started getting sour, I thought negatively of my husband constantly. I focused on his faults and judged him. One day when I was talking (or shall I say complaining) to the Lord about him, He sternly instructed me never to complain to Him about my husband again. Instead, I was to consider my own part in the matter, and if I did wrong, repent and apologize to my husband. If I found I didn't do anything wrong, then I was to make certain I continued treating him right, and the Lord Himself would deal with him.

I didn't like that instruction at all, but I obeyed to the best of my ability at the time. As I continued to grow stronger in the knowledge and understanding of God's Word, I came to see that our ability to communicate with and receive from the Lord is connected to our love walk with others. After all, God is love,[121] and love is the language He respects and responds to. I learned that it is for my own good to treat others right, even when they treat me wrong, because it keeps God on my side and gives satan no opportunity to harm.[122]

I heard a rumor about a leader. Later when I saw a picture of him, negative feelings of disrespect came over me. Thank God I knew better than to nurture those thoughts and feelings. Instead, I quickly rebuked them and prayed blessings over him. That resistance kept me from judging him based on a rumor and kept me obedient to God's command to love instead of joining with the adversary to condemn him.

SPIRIT OF DEFILEMENT

> *See to it that no one falls short of God's grace; that*
> *no root of resentment springs up and causes trouble,*
> *and by it many be defiled...* (Hebrews 12:15 AMP)

Over the years, I have been asked and given authority to pray for certain marriages and families. It is always a privilege to do so. At one time, a couple was having trouble communicating. Strife ensued and lingered in the husband. He either withheld conversation completely or said hurtful things to her. When I talked to her, I noticed a lot of sadness in her voice. The negative words were really taking a toll on her, and she didn't know how to reconcile with him, since he was being so hostile towards her.

It came to me that his ill treatment was due to negative thoughts about her. Then a strong anointing to pray for them came on me, and I discerned a 'spirit of defilement' was speaking in his ear. I have known that spirits interject defiling thoughts, and as far as I recall, I had not heard of a spirit with that label before. So I canceled the assignment of the spirit and commanded it to leave him in Jesus Name. Then I released the ministering angels to speak good things about her to him. Shortly, their relationship was restored.[123]

Not long after that, I was asked by a mother to pray for her son who was being very disrespectful and lying to her–so much that she considered putting him out of the house. As I prayed, I discerned that the root of his problem was also due to a 'spirit of defilement' speaking to him against his mother. There was also a 'lying spirit' involved. I came against those spirits, canceled their assignment and invoked ministering angels to speak good thoughts to him about his mom. Shortly, that relationship was also restored.

As I thought about those experiences, I recalled negative communication problems in my own marriage years ago. At times, I had bad thoughts about my husband, but they were almost nothing compared to the negative things that he said to me during certain seasons. I now believe that during the hostile times, a 'spirit of defilement' was certainly involved. I'm also certain that if I knew then what I know now, our married life would have been very different, for I would have taken authority over that spirit like I did for the other couple.

I understand that every disagreement or argument is not due to a spirit, since the weaknesses in our souls and bodies alone cause problems in relationships. However, I do believe that when things become hostile, and love turns to hatefulness and bitter strife, evil spirits have taken advantage of the weaknesses and entered into the mix.[124] That's when we need to exercise our authority to kick them out and release our ministering angels to counter satan's work.[125]

RESIST WHEN THE DEVIL KNOCKS

"I tell you the truth, whatever you forbid on earth will be forbidden in heaven, and whatever you permit on earth will be permitted in heaven. (Matthew 18:18 NLT)

On February 28, 1998, about three o'clock in the morning, I heard a persistent knocking at the door. It woke me up, but I was very groggy. Did I really hear that? It sounded very real, yet it was different. I propped up on one arm and listened to see if I would hear the knock again. Suddenly, I sensed a very eerie feeling in the atmosphere, which I recognized as the presence of an evil spirit. Then I had a short vision of the front door and saw one huge hairy leg step through the closed door. The leg reminded me of the fictional Bigfoot creature. Now I understood who had knocked, and I needed to resist to keep it from entering my home. With that understanding, I immediately began to proclaim boldly, "No! No you don't!" That's all I said before the leg disappeared. The vision ended, and the eerie presence left.

I had never experienced anything like that before, and I didn't understand what had actually happened. As I pondered it, I asked the Lord why the spirit knocked on the door. What's more, why did it start to enter when I didn't invite it in? Shortly, He answered me with this insight.

In essence, He explained that the spirit knocked because it needed permission to enter. The devil can't just come in and harm anyone whenever he wants; he must have a legitimate cause.[126] He needs permission, the Lord said. That's why, whether we know it or not, he always knocks if he doesn't already have permission through our own words or actions. Since he's an outlaw, when I didn't answer, he took it as silent permission to enter. Because he's a thief, he must be resisted to keep him out. In other words, if I do nothing, I allow the enemy to carry out his plan.

I'm not saying that there aren't other reasons as to why we get attacked with problems. Jesus Himself said that in this world we will have trouble, but we can remain cheerful for He has overcome for us.[127] One thing that's for sure is that satan attacks weak areas of our souls, bodies, and lives. He also orchestrates situations and sets up snares to create weak areas that he can access then or later.

He is a strategist, and since he's been at it for millennia, he's very good at it.

The Lord further explained that the devil has many ways of knocking that most people ignore or altogether miss. To help me understand what He meant, He brought to my mind two experiences I had had several years before.

One day I was washing white clothes while wearing my favorite blue sweater. As I was about to pour in the bleach, a thought came to my mind that I was going to spill it on my sweater. I thought that was ridiculous, knowing how cautious I am with bleach. Yet, despite my cautiousness, somehow the bleach splashed up from the tub onto the sleeve of my sweater. I was heartbroken and confused about the unusual and even unnatural way that it happened, but I just let it go and threw the sweater away.

In another experience I had after that incident, I was relaxing in bed one evening. I had a little makeshift table next to my bed with a small glass of grape juice on it. A flash of an image went across my mind of the juice spilling on my nice house shoes underneath the table. I dismissed it as foolishness, but almost immediately I somehow lost my balance as I leaned over to get the juice. I hit the table, dismantling it and spilling the juice on my shoes just as I had seen. Again, I was dismayed and confused as to how that happened, for it was so unnatural.

I had already learned from those and other experiences that I need to denounce and resist those kinds of thoughts and images from the enemy because he uses them against us. Now the Lord was giving me further revelation that these and other methods are satan's way of knocking to get permission to carry out his plan.

Now, I am even more determined not to be passive anymore. I must stay on the alert and be proactive. I now also practice keeping my emotions in check to avoid creating an opening through which the enemy can enter my life.

I have personally discovered that saying "No, in Jesus' Name" to the devil and firmly resisting his attempts to enter in and wreak havoc must become a way of life in order to live free. I know there are some situations that are more complicated, and help may be needed to dislodge him from his position if he has gained an advantage in our lives. However, resisting him firmly is always appropriate, even when we have unwittingly opened the door to let him in. With this in mind, I start by boldly saying, "No, I don't receive..." to every negative thing that attempts to enter my life. Then I seek the Lord for any further instructions to see if anything more is necessary to defeat my enemy.

> *saying "No, in Jesus' Name" to the devil and firmly resisting his attempts to enter in and wreak havoc must become a way of life in order to live free.*

FOCUS ON THE GOOD

> *And now, dear brothers and sisters, one final thing. Fix your thoughts on what is true, and honorable, and right, and pure, and lovely, and admirable. Think about things that are excellent and worthy of praise.* (Philippians 4:8 NLT)

Questions, questions, questions! Who doesn't have questions at times about why bad things happen or why good things didn't happen as we thought they should. The enemy is masterful at playing games with our minds when things don't go as we want or think they should. We have to be ready to shut him down with the Sword of the Spirit (which is the Word of God that we believe and speak) and the Word that we live by, or he will win, and we will lose.[128]

I have experienced faltering faith, discouragement, and even hopeless moments because I focused too much on the negative situations that I faced and lost sight of God's goodness and His Word which has all the answers. To keep my peace and stay in faith without doubting or complaining, I must keep my focus on what I know about God and to trust His faithfulness when I don't understand.

With that in mind, in every situation, whether good or bad, I fix my mind on the Truth that I know. I know that God is good, and His mercy endures forever to me! God is always faithful. God loves me and all mankind, and His love never fails![129] God is not the one who steals, kills and destroys His children. That's always the devil's work.[130] God is for me, and He shows me how to be more than a conqueror in every situation I face.[131] God's plans for me are all good and lead to an abundant, victorious life![132]

I've learned I must keep these things in mind and magnify the love and goodness of God while denouncing the works of the enemy in order to stay at peace and obey God's instructions to:

> *Rejoice always, pray continually, give thanks in all circumstances; for this is God's will for you in Christ Jesus.* (1 Thessalonians 5:16-18 NIV)

6

SPIRITUAL, MENTAL AND PHYSICAL HEALTH

Now, may the God of peace and harmony set you apart, making you completely holy. And may your entire being– spirit, soul, and body–be kept completely flawless in the appearing of our Lord Jesus, the Anointed One.
1 Thessalonians 5:23 TPT

EAT RIGHT

Over the years, the Lord has taught me through the Word and through many teachings how to stay healthy spiritually, mentally and physically. Good health in every area is all about what we take into our spirits, minds and bodies on a consistent basis.

SPIRITUAL HEALTH

> *...discipline yourself for the purpose of godliness [keeping yourself spiritually fit].* (1 Timothy 4:7 AMP)

Jesus, who taught in parables so we can understand spiritual truths through the natural parallels, called Himself the Bread of Life. He told us that we must eat His Flesh and drink His Blood to have eternal life. Until the Holy Spirit revealed to me the spiritual meaning, these sayings were as confusing to my mind when I read them as they apparently were to the people to whom He was physically speaking.

The simple explanation is unveiled through understanding that Jesus is the Word made flesh (although there's nothing simple about that),[133] and He purchased our eternal life with His Blood, for life is in the Blood.[134] Therefore, to eat His flesh is to eat the Word–through reading, studying and doing the Word–and to drink His Blood is to receive the Sacrifice of His shed Blood as the payment for our eternal life as well as receiving its power to work in us and for us.[135]

Early in my Christian walk, two very well-known ministers fell into sin and disgrace in the same season. Their failures caused me to question my ability to make it, seeing that they didn't make it. I was still learning what it took to overcome deep rooted issues that caused me to struggle in my life and marriage. The Lord assured me that I could stay faithful to Him as I continued to study and do His Word while drawing close to Him in thanksgiving, praise and worship. In fact, we are given instructions throughout the Word on how to remain strong in our faith and stay faithful to our Lord. Later I found this scripture that released me from all fears of falling away:

> *Now all glory to God, who is able to keep you from falling away and will bring you with great joy into his glorious presence without a single fault.* (Jude 1:24 NLT)

Throughout the years, I have witnessed many Christians receive freedom in Jesus and profess loyalty to follow God yet turn back to their old sinful ways. For some, it was their way of handling the pressures of life. In my quest to stay faithful to God and not allow life's pressures to overwhelm me, the Lord showed me that joy was my answer.

He spoke this Word to me in August 2003:

> *"Rise up rejoicing in the morning. Lie down rejoicing at night, and rejoice all day in between. Rejoice, rejoice, rejoice! Let the joy of the Lord fill your heart continually."*

When I gratefully praise the Lord, He responds with His wonderful Presence. His joy fills my soul, and I receive strength in my inner self. As a result, I am refreshed and experience freedom from the stresses of life.[136]

Over the years, I keep progressing in my faith, and I'm finding the joy of the Lord does indeed give me strength in times of weakness and is good for my health.[137]

My faith grows stronger and stronger as I study, learn and understand more about God through His Word.[138] As a result, I no longer waver with thoughts of not making it all the way to the end. Instead, the more I get to know Him, the more confident I am of His love and tender care for me and others. I feel secure in His love and peace.

the more I get to know Him, the more confident I am of His love and tender care for me and others.

I am well aware that any of us can be like the church of Ephesus, who left their first love and needed to repent to be restored.[139] However, leaving our first love is not as likely to happen as long as we continue doing what the Lord told us to do in order to stay faithful to Him. I make every effort to keep Him first in my life through constant fellowship with Him in reading my Bible, praying, and spending time with Him daily. I give Him my attention and devotion, and He responds with His Presence of joy and peace flooding my soul. What a pleasure to start my day with Him, end it with Him, and hang out with Him all day long!

MENTAL HEALTH

> *Grace to you and peace [inner calm and spiritual well-being] from God our Father and the Lord Jesus Christ.* (1 Corinthians 1:3 AMP)

I never saw myself as having a mental health problem in my younger days, but looking back over my life, I can see that for many years I fit perfectly into today's narrative of the escalating crisis of mental illness. I regularly dealt with depression, suicidal thoughts and other tormenting thoughts that made me feel worthless.

From my earliest memories, I was weighed down with heaviness of heart, and for many years I lived in that place. To me it was normal—painful, but normal. I didn't know that my thoughts of rejection, self-abasement and uselessness fed the hopelessness and depression that I hated so much. Sadly, it didn't get much better as I grew into adulthood for my thoughts remained almost completely negative and self-defeating.

After my salvation, I continued to struggle with oppressive thoughts and feelings until I learned enough of the Word of God and grew strong enough to resist the thoughts that pulled me low. I am learning to recognize the enemy at the onset and not allow oppressive thoughts a chance to work against my mind and body. Furthermore, the Lord exhorted me to be on the alert and immediately resist the smallest inkling of down-hearted thoughts of any kind, including discouragement, frustration and fear. I was not to give such feelings a moment's attention, keeping in mind they are ALWAYS from the enemy. I now see these as fiery darts from the enemy that I must resist with my shield of faith. The Word calls this fighting the good fight of faith.[140]

I know the only way I can fight a spiritual enemy is with the spiritual weapons described in the Word of God like Jesus used in the wilderness with satan.[141] Keeping the door closed to the enemy and open to the Lord takes continual watchfulness and confession of the Word because I am still overcoming past mistakes and unresolved issues in my soul. He showed me that if I am to be a victor instead of a victim, I must not only repent, but also *let go* of those memories and go forward in confidence in His love and forgiveness. I purpose to do what He said to me in August 2003:

> *"No more regrets! No more looking back in doubt about today because of what you did wrong yesterday. No more allowing wrong imaginations to stay in your mind even for two seconds. Cast them down in the first second."*

Fix Your Mind on the Peace Giver

> *"Peace I leave with you. My peace I give to you. I do not give to you as the world gives. Don't let your heart be troubled or fearful.* (John 14:27 CSB)

Scripture exhorts us to look to Jesus and follow His example. To endure the Cross, He focused on the joy that would come from His Sacrifice.[142] In like manner, we focus on the joy of receiving the Lord's victory that He won for us, so we won't lose hope and give up because of the pressures of life. I have certainly found this to be necessary in order to keep resisting and overcoming illnesses, troubles, and satan's attempts to revisit me with past bondages.

To live in constant peace was only a dream to me when I first learned the Scripture:

> *You will keep him in perfect peace, Whose mind is stayed on You, Because he trusts in You.* (Isaiah 26:3 NKJV)

As I have grown in my relationship with the Lord, it is no longer an unattainable dream but a work in progress. I've learned that whenever I find my peace being disturbed, I've allowed some peace-stealing thought to slip through my defenses instead of guarding my mind and casting it down. This happens especially when I'm under pressure. In these pressure situations, I often hear the Lord gently speak to my heart, *"Eyes on Me,"* and I'm alerted to focus on Jesus and the Word, cast down the negative thoughts, put my guard back up and regain my peace.

whenever I find my peace being disturbed, I've allowed some peace-stealing thought to slip through my defenses instead of guarding my mind and casting it down.

Jesus warned us that in this life we are going to face troubles, trials, distress and frustration.[143] We can be certain the enemy will see to that. Jesus exhorts us to stay cheerful through them all because He has overcome them for us. Keeping our eyes fixed on Him makes that possible.

PHYSICAL HEALTH

> ..."*HE HIMSELF TOOK OUR INFIRMITIES [upon Himself] AND CARRIED AWAY OUR DISEASES.*" (Matthew 8:17 AMP)

After I studied Jesus' provision for healing enough to believe and receive multiple healings for myself and my children, He instructed me to make Him our Doctor for every physical need. This actually became necessary because my husband's drug addiction consumed practically all of our money, and we could no longer afford doctors. By then I had gained enough understanding to know that the moment something tries to come upon my body–whether sickness or pain of any kind–not to analyze it, but immediately to proclaim my healing in accordance with what the Word says, and to rebuke that which is attempting to take away my health. In other words, to zealously stand firm against the curse of sickness and disease and to receive all that Jesus paid for us to have, not allowing the high price He paid for my personal health to be wasted.[144]

God's Medicine

> *My son, pay attention to my words and be willing*
> *to learn; Open your ears to my sayings. Do not*
> *let them escape from your sight; Keep them in the*
> *center of your heart. For they are life to those who*
> *find them, And healing and health to all their flesh.*
> (Proverbs 4:20-22 AMP)

This world is full of germs, viruses, toxins and cursed things that affect everyone in some measure. Because of this, I believe everyone may need medical attention at some point to maintain health. The Good News for Christians is that we get to choose whether we obtain our medical help from man, from God, or from both. I have chosen God as my Doctor, and by His grace, He helps me overcome sickness and stay healthy.

Just as you must follow the doctor's orders to get healing results, likewise, it takes the same kind of focus and diligence to follow God's instructions to receive healing through His Word. Like taking natural medicine, I take healing Scriptures as my medicine through believing and confessing them in a personal way.

We have been healed of everything from small pains to major illnesses. My young children (before they reached their teens) were almost always instantly healed, but I've never personally experienced an instant healing. For me it usually takes the good fight of faith, but healing always comes because Jesus won our victory long ago.[145]

Our God has provided supernatural healing for us through several means–laying on of hands, the prayer of faith, anointing with oil, and confessing (agreeing with and receiving) healing Scriptures.[146] My pathway to healing is usually through praying the prayer of faith and confessing healing Scriptures. Confession of God's Word for healing has worked for me in the likeness of Jeremiah 23:29 NKJV:

> *"Is not My word like a fire?" says the LORD, "And like a hammer that breaks the rock in pieces?..."*

Some attacks against our bodies and lives are not instantly removed with prayer, and we must remain steadfast in believing and speaking the Word that promises us the answer to our problem. The reason I confess Scriptures is: 1) to affirm my belief that what I prayed will manifest, 2) to resist harassing thoughts of doubt and unbelief, and 3) to resist other attacks of the enemy meant to hinder my stand of faith. As I stated earlier,[147] I liken the consistent speaking (confessing) the Word to be like a spiritual hammer that is breaking (resisting) the enemy's work every time it is spoken with faith, and undoing his work in Jesus' Name,[148] thus removing the hindrance to our healing so the answer can manifest.[149] The Word of God says we are blessed, we are healed and we are delivered.[150] I learned my part is to take the Word by faith and to enforce our victory by resisting all opposition.

That's what I did when I resisted the spirits of hate and insanity that tried to force themselves on me. I kept declaring the Word to enforce my Redemption and my deliverance from the evil one. After a short time of boldly speaking the Word, both spirits left me.[151]

Furthermore, I have learned over the years that I can maintain my health by daily releasing my faith through believing and speaking[152] certain healing Scriptures to keep my body strong instead of waiting to get sick and then giving attention to praying for healing.

In Chapter Two, I also shared that the Lord helped me to avoid sickness by leading me to confess healing Scriptures over myself beforehand. Following His instructions, I confessed Scriptures twice daily for two and a half months until one morning the Lord spoke to my heart, *"That which was planted is dissolved and rooted out of your body."* He never told me what had been rooted out of me; I just knew whatever it was had been thwarted so it could not harm me.[153]

On another note, I believe God intends for us to use all the natural resources He put in the earth to help us maintain good health. For instance, He put healing in our plant life.[154]

In 2020, when COVID hit, the Lord instructed me to build up and keep my immune system boosted with certain vitamins and minerals for that purpose. Instead of occasionally taking Vitamin C and Echinacea to counter a cold symptom, I started taking them daily, while adding Vitamin D and zinc. These add to my nourishment and help my body fight off harmful invasions that cause sickness and disease.

I'm grateful that our Great Physician gives us the understanding–through giving wisdom to doctors, through His Word and by His Spirit–that we need to address the natural and spiritual things that can steal our health. There are many physical problems that require medical treatment or supernatural healing to solve them. Some things are simple to cure; some are not.

A good example of something that can be easily cured is the

common problem of dehydration. It can become a very serious problem under certain conditions. Many years ago, my husband told me of an incident where he suffered severe consequences from dehydration while running track to qualify for his college football team. He had purposely refrained from eating and drinking water so he wouldn't exceed the weight limit. To make matters worse, it was an extremely hot summer day, and he was pushing himself to make the time limit on his track run. He passed out during the run and was taken to the university's infirmary. While there, he had a near-death experience, but due to praying parents and the mercy of God, he survived.

I have had a number of varying experiences with individuals, including myself, who also suffered physical problems due to dehydration. None were as dramatic as my husband's, but in some cases, unnecessary medical treatments were given because we didn't understand the root of the problem. That's why I believe God wants me to share some of my experiences to warn others to learn and watch for symptoms of dehydration–especially in the children. While some cases I have personally encountered were simple to diagnose, other cases were more complicated, but the Lord revealed the answer.

The Water Cure

Some statistics say that 75 percent of Americans are chronically dehydrated, and a good percentage are admitted to the hospital.[155] According to my own personal experiences, I have no doubt in the validity of that statistic.

Taking that statistic into account, I encourage everyone not to be too hasty to seek professional medical attention when dealing with simple symptoms of dehydration, but instead to investigate the water intake and treat the symptoms with water first if possible. I have experienced several situations over the years that looked like they needed medical attention, but all it took to regain health was to increase hydration.

1) Loss of Consciousness

A few years ago, one of my daughters started passing out for seemingly no reason. She'd be fine one moment, and suddenly she'd just lose consciousness for a few minutes–sometimes in the middle of a conversation. It seemed serious, but I sought the Lord for an answer, and He said, "water and salt." From then on, every time it happened, which was quite frequent during that season, we shook her awake and gave her water to drink and salt to eat, and she regained her strength.

Even though she passed out the day before our vacation to Florida, we went ahead with our scheduled trip. After we arrived, she started passing out in an elevator. Her husband and I calmly assured the onlooking tourists that everything was okay as we propped her up to keep her from dropping to the floor. We didn't want anyone panicking and calling an ambulance for liability purposes. Thank God we were able to help her walk off the elevator to a seat and quickly got her water and salt to revive her. When we returned home, she finally started hydrating properly and that season passed.

2) Vomiting and Feeling Sickly

It was my second daughter's Prom night. The Christian school's prom was a dinner with no dancing. The teens weren't ready for the evening to end, so my daughter called to see if she could bring a few friends over for an impromptu afterparty. I said okay and watched in apprehension as a mass of teens trailed into the house, filling the living room. Fortunately, my future son-in-law was visiting and had his DJ equipment in his vehicle, so he provided the music, while we adults enjoyed watching them dance and have fun.

One young man was a very good dancer and was especially energetic. After a time of high energy dancing, he started feeling sick and disoriented. While he was in the bathroom vomiting, my oldest daughter and I prayed and, inspired by the Holy Spirit, said almost in unison, "water!" He needed water! We gave him a drink, and he started feeling better. We gave him more water, and he began feeling normal. Then we instructed him on his need to drink plenty because he was such an energetic person. I'm sure our advice was especially helpful because he shared that on another occasion he had gone to the Emergency Room for the same symptoms. No doubt he was given the needed treatment with an IV–water and salt–and was sent home with a large financial bill.

3) Dizziness

We had quite a challenge working with my nine-year-old grandson to drink water. Even though we made it clear that the health issues he was having were due to lack of sufficient water, he still resisted. During one season, his teacher frequently called his mother in her concern for his dizziness while in school. So when we were traveling together and he pulled out pills to treat another dizzy spell (after refusing to drink water), in indignation I took the pills and insisted he drink up or else....

I kept the pills during our three-day trip and replaced them with water. After a short time, he stopped complaining about dizziness and asking for the pills. I gladly admit that he never got those pills back.

4) Heat Exhaustion

During the next four years, we continued to work with my grandson to encourage him to drink the appropriate amount of water for proper hydration, even more so now that he's running track. However, it has still been a struggle to get him to do so.

He's a good athlete, and he's fast! In fact, he's one of the fastest on the team. So it's no surprise that at the State Track Meet, in addition to running the 100m and 200m, he also ran anchor for the 4X100m and 4X200m relays and took first place in all of them.

When we went to congratulate him and say goodbye at the end of his last race, we found him sitting on the ground very overheated and intensely struggling to breathe. Of course, he admitted he had not drunk the amount of water he was instructed to drink. But thank God, through the teamwork between the coaching staff and family praying for him, drenching him with cold water while making him drink a lot, and rubbing him with ice packs, he revived. Although when he stood up, it's no surprise that he felt a little dizzy. However, the good thing that came from the experience is that he said he no longer needs us to inspire him to drink water; he is now motivated to drink on his own.

5) Headache

It was also a challenge getting the need to drink enough water across to my granddaughter since her definition of drinking 'plenty of water' wasn't much more than a few sips. However, her mom and I kept working with her, which included showing her articles on dehydration and its symptoms to convince her to drink more.

Whenever she complains about having a headache, we evaluate her water intake for the day and always find that it is extremely deficient. Then we give her the simple cure–water–and the headache complaint ceases.

6) Abdominal Pain

After I left my mother's home and throughout my twenties,

my eating habits were not conducive to good health. To make things worse, I didn't like drinking water, and I didn't think I could enjoy life without having a soda with every meal. As a result, I started having health issues–lots of bladder infections, often feeling very yucky and at times having a sharp pain in my lower abdominal.

It came to the point where the occasional pain got so bad that I went to the doctor for help. After visiting him several times with no answers, he suggested exploratory surgery to find a diagnosis. So I was admitted into the hospital, and he drilled four holes in my abdomen to search for the problem. He found nothing wrong, and the pain kept coming.

Finally, when I reached my thirties, I started listening to the Lord about my eating when my health declined even more. During that time, God dealt with my food choices and had me change to whole grain and organic foods. He also led me to deep cleanse my body. While detoxing, I noticed that if I didn't daily flush my system soon enough of the toxins that were being pulled from my fatty tissues back into my bloodstream, I would get those same sharp pains in my lower abdomen. From then on, if I ate even a small amount of something that was toxic to me, I almost immediately felt the same pain, which would be relieved with lots of water. It was only then that I realized the reason why the doctor found nothing during the exploratory surgery years ago. Since toxins apparently settle in my lower abdomen, I was obviously dehydrated and suffering from toxic overload because I didn't drink enough water to flush the toxins out.

The connection between the abdominal pain and insufficient water was further verified during a training event at our church camp. After a light meal, we met in the chapel. Sharp abdominal pain started escalating until it was difficult to sit in the meeting. I was occasionally drinking from my water bottle when the Lord spoke to my heart, *Chug your water.* I quickly drank it, got another water bottle and started drinking it. The more I drank, the more the pain diminished until it all left.

I now make certain to drink the recommended daily amount of water for my weight, and I'm doing the best that I know how to help my loved ones do the same.

7

MAKE READY FOR JESUS RETURN

Let us rejoice and exalt him and give him glory,
because the wedding celebration of the Lamb has
come. And his bride has made herself ready.
Revelation 19:7 TPT

Shortly after I was Born Again, I began hearing teachings about Jesus' return for His Bride–a Glorious Church of unified Believers–and His charge to prepare ourselves for His coming. Since then, I've been compelled by the Lord to study the subject and to pray for Believers to awaken from spiritual sleep and do what is necessary to be ready for His return.[156] In the process, He has allowed me to go through many situations in which I have learned to face and overcome weaknesses and issues that need to be cleansed from my soul–the burdens and sins that easily hinder and trip me up.[157] As a result, part of my calling is to pray for the Body of Christ, while inspiring and helping others to overcome so we will make ourselves ready to be the beautiful Bride for whom Jesus is returning.[158]

In fact, in 1990, the Lord instructed me to name my ministry, "Overcoming Life Ministries." At the time I hadn't overcome very much so I thought that name was not very fitting for me. Over the years, however, He has led me to overcome many things, and I will be overcoming till the end of my time on this earth and helping others to do the same.

Scripture says we Christians will be required to give an account for our lives at the Judgment Seat of Christ. Jesus told a parable depicting this.[159] As in the parable, we will give an account for what He entrusted us to accomplish as part of the Body of Christ, and He'll reward us accordingly. Because we are redeemed and brought into the Kingdom of God at a very costly price–the Sacrifice of Jesus' Precious Blood–we are given a charge to glorify God in our bodies.[160] We are commanded to love one another as He has loved us.[161] We are also instructed to live by faith, unite together in the unity of the Spirit through peace and overcome evil with good.[162] We will answer to our Lord Jesus at His judgment Seat for these things and for our personal assignments.

I have heard many Christians, including myself, express their desire to hear our Lord Jesus greet them at their homegoing with the same greeting given to the servant in the parable. He said, *"Well done, good and faithful servant."*[163] However, I haven't heard much discussion about the Christians' judgment. I have talked to some Christians who knew about the judgment of sinners at the Great White Throne, but they didn't know about the Judgment Seat of Christ where Christians will be required to give an account. We will all receive our due payment for how we conduct ourselves in this life.[164]

Sometimes believers fail to consider how important God's plan and purpose for our lives is to God. This lack of understanding could cause us to make wrong choices that do not honor Him and could even thwart His plan for us. He wants us to live triumphant lives, as trophies of Christ's victory, and spread the knowledge of God's goodness everywhere we go.[165]

Sometimes when dealing with painful situations I'd rather avoid, I am tempted to disobey God's personal instructions and to dishonor His plan for my life until I stop to remember the awesome things the Lord has done for me. I realize what I am trying to avoid is puny and insignificant compared to His Great Sacrifice for me.[166] I'm also reminded of what Jesus said in another parable about us giving an account when He returns.

> *For everyone to whom much is given, from him much will be required; and to whom much has been committed, of him they will ask the more.* (Luke 12:48 NKJV)

This Scripture causes me to consider how much the Lord has given us to overcome our enemy and fulfill our purpose. We have the Holy Spirit to guide us, the fruit of the Spirit to empower us, and angelic hosts to help us.[167] The abundance of grace and truth that came through our Lord Jesus has given us unmerited favor with God and has empowered us to accomplish all that's required of us no matter what we face. His provision annuls any excuses to slack off from following God's will because Jesus makes difficult situations easy to bear when we follow His plan and depend on His strength.[168]

Therefore, I have taken the Apostle Paul's advice very seriously to examine myself to make certain my faith is genuine, and my actions are acceptable to God.[169] For instance, I had to endure hardship in my marriage for a season while my husband dealt with drug addiction. With God's help, I had to be very intentional to release unconditional love and forgiveness to him when none was returned. Later, I had to change my way of dealing with my children as they grew into their teenage and adult stages. I had to learn how to treat them as mature individuals and not frustrate them with my parenting. I received their feedback to help me judge myself, and I made changes accordingly. Doing so keeps me in right relationship with them as I love them the way God loves us.[170] The Word of God says if we judge ourselves, we will not be judged and disciplined by the Lord.[171] I prefer to be corrected now and trust to be found faithful when He comes.

HONOR GOD AND BE HONORED

...those who honor Me I will honor... (1 Samuel
2:30 NKJV)

One of the hardest things I've had to do as a Christian is to give
my will completely over to the will of God. In the very beginning of
my Christian walk, it was easy because I was so elated to experience
the freedom from the darkness and load of sin that I once carried.
In appreciation and honor to Him, I gladly gave my whole self
over to my new Lord and Savior, or so I thought. That is, until I
started learning the Word and the requirements to live a godly life,
especially to love others unconditionally. Then I faced the hard
things of my new life–forgive, don't judge, apologize when I didn't
want to, speak kindly or not at all, and more! I found I had to make
some choices daily, and they were my choices alone to make. It
became clear that even though Jesus is my Lord, I am free to do His
will as laid out in the Word or to do my own thing. He won't force
any of us. He guides, and we choose to follow or not.[172]

I know it will require following His plan and not our own in
order to honor Him so that one day we can hear Him recognize
our faithfulness. So I've chosen to give my all to Jesus–according
to all that I understand about His Word and will for me–and let
Him truly be the Lord of all my life. As I learn more, I will give
more; I choose to give up my way and follow His Way. I knew
then and continue to know now that I cannot accomplish such
surrender in my own strength. In order to live out my decision,
I release my faith daily to receive God's help to strengthen and
guide me.

I know the major thing I need daily is wisdom. In Proverbs
it says God's wisdom is more valuable than jewels or gold.[173]
Therefore, I continually ask for it, and believe I receive it according
to James 1:5, where it says the Lord will give it to me when I ask. I
know I must have His wisdom to follow His plan and accomplish

His will. Yielding to His Lordship puts me in the position to receive it from Him.[174] Jesus said it is the Father's good pleasure to give us His Kingdom–including all the blessings and wisdom we need to prosper in every area and finish our race strong. Learning the Father's heart to affectionately care for and provide for His children has caused me to be able to relax and trust Him to meet all my needs and has given me much peace.[175]

After Jesus told a parable about our need to pray and never give up, He asked the question, *"...when the Son of Man comes, will He really find faith on the earth?"*[176] Since He touched my heart with this Scripture over thirty years ago, I have been on a quest to be found with faith at His coming. I have come to trust Him more and more, following His guidance even when I don't understand the purpose. One of my most notable experiences of His loving, watchful care involved my first car.

By 1983, my ten-year-old yellow Ford Mustang II was well used and ready to be replaced. Even so, my husband wanted to wait until the end of the year to get our new car. The Mustang still drove okay so there didn't appear to be any need to rush. Yet, I strongly sensed in my heart not to wait three months but to get another vehicle soon. I wanted a Volvo, but he said "No," because a friend advised him the maintenance was too costly. Therefore, I prayed and trusted God for us to have the right car at the right time.

About two weeks after our discussion to wait on buying the car, my husband surprised me one Saturday morning when he wanted to go look at cars–although he made it clear that we were only looking and not buying until later. He surprised me again when he pulled into a Volvo dealership. They had a nice new 1984 beige Volvo with about 800 miles on it. The price was greatly discounted because it was used as a test-drive car. I felt in my heart that it was the car for us. Then I got another sweet surprise when my husband agreed with my appeal to him that we shouldn't pass up the good deal, and we purchased it.

They needed to clean it since it was used to test-drive. Therefore, we were to pick it up the next day. Another big surprise happened on the way home from the dealership. As soon as we turned into our neighborhood, the Mustang–that we had just traded in for our new car–suddenly became unsteerable. We coasted to the side of the road, got out and looked underneath to find the axle had broken in two. [We had decided at the last minute to trade it in instead of keeping it as an extra vehicle.] Needless to say, we praised God as we walked the rest of the way to our home about a half mile away. The next day we picked up our new car, and they came and towed away their broken Mustang.

Another experience of God's loving care is when His guidance kept me in a position to help my adult children when they needed me.

In 2009, I started planning to downsize to a one bedroom apartment when my last child was about to leave home, but the Lord spoke to my heart not to move. I knew I would have a decrease in income in a few months, and it would be a struggle to pay the rent. However, His instructions were clear, so I abandoned my plan and stayed in my three bedroom duplex. I got a part-time job for extra income to cover expenses. About a year later, my second daughter and her baby boy moved back home when her military husband deployed overseas. I was very grateful that I had followed God's direction. For about two years, I was blessed to help her raise my first grandchild. I was even more appreciative for God's guidance when my youngest daughter moved back home and joined us.

There is no way for me to calculate how much peace and ease it has brought to me to give my life completely into the hands of God. I believe this is the ease and rest that Jesus offered when He invited us to come to Him, learn His ways and get help to live free from the burdens of life. He promised to give rest to our souls.[177] After all, He is the Lord of Peace, and His wonderful peace is available to everyone who receives Jesus as Lord and Savior.[178]

The Lord spoke to my heart in morning prayer in April 2000:

> *"Give Me your time, and I'll give you priceless things in return. I'll give you ideas, concepts and insights. I'll give you the way out of your present situation. I'll give you manna from Heaven that will satisfy your soul. I'll give you priceless gifts that you cannot buy."*[179]

I am determined to keep increasing my time with the Lord–in His Word, in prayer and intimate fellowship–in order to receive everything I need to help me honor Him, overcome in life and be ready for Jesus' return.

DON'T REJECT THE WORD

> *...with a sensitive spirit we absorb God's Word, which has been implanted within our nature, for the Word of Life has power to continually deliver us.* (James 1:21 TPT)

I recall a minister once saying that there is one thing stronger than the Word of God. Then he quoted and expounded on this Scripture:

> *Thus you nullify the Word of God by your tradition that you have handed down. And you do many things like that."* (Mark 7:13 NIV)

So it is possible to be so stuck in our traditions that the Word of God, which has all the answers, is made ineffective on our behalf and won't work for us! This can be very serious when it is clearly revealed that the tradition contradicts the Word.

When I gave my life to Jesus and started studying the Word

and learning from Bible teachers and ministers, I discovered personal viewpoints and traditions that needed to be changed in my thinking. At first some of God's holy ways didn't appeal to me–such as to love someone mistreating me, to shut my mouth and not try to prove myself to be right (which usually led to an argument), or to submit when I didn't want to, etc. As I grew and learned more about God's love and desire to bless us, I came to understand God's thoughts and His ways always bring freedom.[180] Then I began to embrace all His Word, even when I don't fully understand it.

I personally witnessed a friend completely reject God's blessing in order to stay with his denomination's stand against God's provision for healing.

One afternoon, many years ago, a close friend of ours came to visit. He said that he had some kind of painful problem with his eyes. I asked if I could pray for him, and he said yes. I prayed and the pain left him. He was shocked—so shocked that he stood there and repeatedly blinked his eyes in disbelief. After what seemed like a long time of blinking, it became clear to me that he was looking for the pain, and he wasn't going to let up until he found it! Finally, after quite a while of blinking and searching, with a sense of accomplishment he exclaimed, "There it is!"

Like Jesus, I marveled at his unbelief![181] I understood that he was part of a denomination that doesn't really believe God's gifts of healing are for us today; yet he got healed and rejected it! Observing this made it clear that accepting my prayer was basically a courtesy to me, with no expectancy of any results. I suppose to him it was just a religious act that went crosswise to what he truly believed. Even so, I didn't take it personally because I knew he didn't reject me; he rejected Jesus' Sacrifice for his healing. I'm certain he didn't consider that rejecting Jesus' work of healing grace would cause him to end up with satan's work of more pain.[182]

I believe rejecting God's Word and the provisions it provides for our lives leaves us vulnerable to the enemy's works. Our Lord Jesus has provided an abundantly blessed life for us that overcomes everything that would steal, kill or destroy us in any form, but we can only receive it by our faith.[183]

KEEP A PURE HEART

> *Blessed are the pure in heart, For they shall see God.* (Matthew 5:8 NKJV)

I once thought the above Scripture was only about seeing God when we get to Heaven until I heard a minister explain that it also has to do with our ability to see (discern, have spiritual insight or receive revelation from) God in our lives now. Then I discovered this interpretation of the Scripture:

> *"What bliss you experience when your heart is pure! For then your eyes will open to see more and more of God.* (Matthew 5:8 TPT)

From the beginning of my salvation, the Lord has dealt with me to be selective about that to which I expose my heart in entertainment and to avoid foul language, critical gossip, judgmental conversations and any perverse thing, because these things pollute the heart and hinder our relationship with Him. Of course, this also includes not polluting the heart by indulging in unbridled sin and willful disobedience.[184] Over the years, I have progressively gotten better and wiser at guarding my heart, understanding that the affections of my heart determine the course of my life.[185]

I make it a point not to violate my conscience with things that would pollute my heart and make me feel condemned before God. That way I won't give any opportunity to the devil to harass me. Most importantly, I want to stay in a place where I have constant fellowship with the Lord and keep my confidence towards God so I can boldly approach His Throne of grace to receive help whenever I need it.[186]

My heart's desire is to shun the things that God hates that are against His character and instead always choose to please Him, by loving what He loves and hating what He hates.[187] For anyone to be successful at doing that will require His help, which comes as we daily yield ourselves to His way and His will. I believe it is possible to live at that level of faith and commitment as we continually fill our hearts with the Word and spend time in His Presence. If the Psalmist–who did not have the Holy Spirit abiding in him as we do–could hide God's Word in his heart so he would not sin against Him, so can we.[188] In fact, His Word is so powerful and His Presence so fulfilling, we can be empowered to not even desire to sin against Him.[189] Of course, that doesn't mean we won't ever mess up or sin, but willful sinning won't be our lifestyle. We'll choose instead to honor God and shun the things that dishonor Him. This is my heart's desire and my everyday goal towards which I'm pressing. I believe this is what it takes to be part of the pure-hearted Bride getting ready for His coming!

COMMIT IT TO GOD

> *Commit to the Lord whatever you do, and he will establish your plans.* (Proverbs 16:3 NIV)

Very early in my Christian life I was drawn to a Scripture that caused me to focus on my need for God's Help.

> *'Not by might nor by power, but by My Spirit,' says the Lord of hosts.* (Zechariah 4:6 NKJV)

I meditated on that Scripture often along with other Scriptures that express our need for dependence on God's strength within us[190] until that Truth saturated my heart and mind. This gave me the understanding that my ability to succeed at anything God leads me to do will require the help of the Holy Spirit. I have found that whenever I struggle with attempting to do God's will, I am trying to do it in my own strength without depending on the grace of God which empowers me.[191] So I have learned to take every task and instruction that the Lord gives me and commit it to Him for His help to carry it out.

He said in His Word that His commandments are not hard or burdensome to keep.[192] I'm sure that's because He expects us to look to Him and depend on our Helper, the Holy Spirit, just as Jesus depended on the Father God to help Him do everything He did when He was here.[193] In the early years of my Christian life, some of His instructions were hard for me because of bondages in my life which I had allowed to control me in times of pressure. Now whenever I face something that I don't know how to do or that seems too big for me, I consider and confess, "*I can do all things through Christ who strengthens me,*"[194] and I get help from the Lord.

It will certainly take God's help for us to make ourselves ready for Jesus' return.[195] I believe He is actively leading us by His Spirit at all times, but we must keep our spiritual ears tuned to hear Him in order to participate in the victory that He always gives.[196] Certainly the Father will answer Jesus' prayer to unite us and cause us to be evidence to the world that Jesus is truly the Son of God.[197] Therefore, in cooperation with His will:

> *...let us go right into the presence of God with sincere hearts fully trusting him. For our guilty consciences have been sprinkled with Christ's blood to make us clean, and our bodies have been washed with pure water. Let us hold tightly without wavering to the hope we affirm, for God can be trusted to keep his promise. Let us think of ways to motivate one*

> *another to acts of love and good works. And let us*
> *not neglect our meeting together, as some people*
> *do, but encourage one another, especially now that*
> *the day of his return is drawing near.* (Hebrews
> 10:22-25 NLT)

LET THE WORD OF GOD DELIVER THE SOUL

> *Therefore, ridding yourselves of all moral filth and*
> *the evil that is so prevalent, humbly receive the*
> *implanted word, which is able to save your souls.*
> *But be doers of the word and not hearers only,*
> *deceiving yourselves.* (James 1:21-22 CSB)

In the early years of my salvation, I experienced a tug of war between my soul and my Born Again spirit when I was faced with things that I didn't want to submit to. It helped me understand the cause of my struggles when I learned that the soul is made up of the mind (intellect), will and emotions (feelings). I needed to renew my mind with God's Word so I could have His Mind on the things that troubled me, submit my will to do His will, and give Him control of my emotions instead of letting them control me.[198]

We are warned in Romans 13 that time is running out, and the day of salvation is near, so we should live our lives reflecting the character of Jesus rather than indulging in evil desires.[199] We can do this because God cleansed our hearts from the nature of sin. Now we are to cleanse our minds and bodies from the acts of sin. It's our choice to take God's Word into our hearts and get free or to be controlled by ungodly desires and urges that hinder our walk with God.[200] Early in my Christian life, I experienced many struggles between resisting ungodly temptations or giving in to my feelings. At times it felt like a war was raging inside of me.

Unfortunately, I sometimes lost the battle when I allowed anger, fear, overeating, depression, etc, to overcome me.

The Lord said to me in 1999, *"It's not possible to overcome the one* (the evil one) *that you yield part of your life to."*[201] I knew He was warning me not to yield to satan as I had done in the past. I understood He was referring to deep-rooted issues from which I had not yet gotten completely free, giving satan the opportunity to take advantage of my weaknesses. I took that to heart and spent more time studying and applying the Word to those areas of my life. I want to be completely free from everything that hinders my walk with God and every sin that once entangled me.[202]

The Lord gave me insight on May 16, 2000, as to why it is so important to be set free. He said:

> *"This is the time of increased Glory and Light in the Body of Christ, and it's the time of increased darkness in the world.[203] In this time of increased darkness, if the darkness is not completely purged out of your soul, it will rise up against you to defeat you."*

He made it clear that I must use all the resources He has placed in my life if I am to overcome in every area. Those resources include specific reading materials and teachings, Godly influences, and most importantly, the Word of God studied, meditated on and confessed.

He also spoke to my heart in February 2012, *"All that Heaven has is ours in Christ, but we will only experience what we receive. We will only be free from what we release."*

One major thing I've learned is that satan attacks the weak places in our souls and bodies. When I look at the sum of my life, I can clearly see that whenever I had been driven towards suicide, anger, hate, and fear, it was because I was weak and susceptible in that area. I'm certain that is one reason why the Lord impressed on my heart that He doesn't want us in a place where nothing or no one ever touches our weaknesses so they remain dormant and hidden. Instead, He wants our weaknesses and bondages exposed so we can let Him remove them.

I volunteer with a ministry that ministers to teenagers. When we found one teen sitting in the lobby waiting for the group session to end, someone asked why she wasn't with the group. She said the last time she attended the teaching made her cry, and she didn't want to cry again. Obviously, the subject matter had touched painful, unresolved issues in her soul, and she didn't want to deal with the pain. I understand her actions because there was a time when I felt the same way. I absolutely didn't want anything to touch those painful areas of deep-rooted issues that I wanted to avoid and not think about. However, over time, every issue was touched through some experience or relationship that put pressure on me, and I had to face the pain and allow God–through His Word and by His Spirit–to deliver me. In the process, He also delivered me from low self-esteem, self-hatred, self-pity, rejection, condemnation and anger. I certainly didn't like dealing with those issues at the time, but after having overcome them, I am so glad I did. Now that I have those major strongholds subdued and under my feet, overcoming life's ongoing problems and pressures has gotten much easier.

The Word of God says Jesus gave His life for the Church so we can be holy and clean through the cleansing power of His Word. This is the glorious Church for whom He is coming.[204] However, we have to cooperate with Him by presenting our bodies to the Lord to do His will, renewing our minds with His Word and allowing it to transform and cleanse us as we do what it says.[205] By the grace of God, we can make ourselves ready for our Lord because the Word says His Bride will be ready when He comes.[206]

OVERCOME THE ENEMY

> *These are the nations that the Lord left in the land to test those Israelites who had not experienced the wars of Canaan. He did this to teach warfare to generations of Israelites who had no experience in battle.* (Judges 3:1-2 NLT)

The Lord made it very clear that He had given Israel the Promised Land, and He would personally drive out their enemies for them. All they had to do was keep His commandments and not serve the enemies' idols or intermarry with them. So He tested them by taking His time to drive them out, in order to see what they would do when faced with the choices put before them while their enemies were still in the land.

Furthermore Judges 3:4 NLT says, *"These people were left to test the Israelites—to see whether they would obey the commands the LORD had given to their ancestors through Moses."*

After studying these Scriptures, the Lord impressed upon my heart that it is a parallel to some of my own past and present experiences, as well as others' experiences for whom I have prayed for over the years. Like Israel, we are surrounded by evil daily, so we constantly get to choose our Lord God over everything the enemy has to offer. In doing so, we get to do what He charged us to do many times throughout the Bible–we get to exalt our God and overcome our enemy.[207]

To help me understand why He leads us through difficulties, He gave me this Word:

> *"I never lead My people into evil, nor do I use evil in any way to reform or to train you. I do send you to dark places where evil is present so you can face it, defeat it, and overcome the evil one that has already been defeated for you.[208] Whenever you*

*are overcome by evil, it is not Me allowing it or
sanctioning it to train or discipline you. It is you
allowing it by not receiving the strength of your
victory that makes you greater than the evil you
face. If I send you into a dark place, then you have
knowledge of how to overcome your defeated foe.
Whether you use the knowledge or not is your test
that you pass or fail. I always require you to use
what you have received from Me."*

Jesus defeated satan, handed us His victory, and He is seated at
the right hand of the Father waiting for us, the Body of Christ, to
enforce His victory and overcome the devil. The Revelation given
to the Apostle John reveals that we will use the knowledge of God
and His Word and overcome our enemy.[209]

COMPLETE THE FAITH TEST

*...so we speak not to please men but to please God,
Who tests our hearts...*(1 Thess 2:4 AMPC)

*My brothers and sisters, be very happy when you
are tested in different ways. You know that such
testing of your faith produces endurance. Endure
until your testing is over. Then you will be mature
and complete, and you won't need anything.* (James
1:2-4 GW)

I have come to understand that the Lord often tests us on big
and small things that He knows need to be overcome so they won't
give opportunity to the devil to hinder or defeat us. Some tests
He has taken me through have come in the form of self-control
and obedience with food, money, loving the unlovely and using

patience while waiting for an answer from Him much longer than I thought was necessary–which is the following case.

In 2013, the Lord instructed me to move. I was still living in my three-bedroom duplex. My two daughters, who had come back home to live with me, had moved out, and I was enjoying being an empty nester. I was happy for the coming move. In preparation, I gave away many things to downsize as I sought Him for the plan. However, He didn't tell me anything except to pack and put the boxes in the garage as I filled them. In obedience, I started packing. Then I started looking for a new home. In the meantime, I gave my 30-day notice to the landlord.

Every time I considered another place to live, I was met with a complete lack of peace in my heart. Since I had purposed to be guided by His peace, I would withdraw.[210] Finally, I realized I was being led by the Lord not to look for a new place but only to pack and trust Him for further instructions. As time passed, I kept mentioning to Him that the 30 days were coming to an end, and I needed the plan. Am I staying in Tulsa? Am I moving home to Tennessee? I wasn't sure what He had in mind for me. I only knew I was open to whatever He had to say, but He wasn't saying anything except to impress upon my heart to keep packing.

It came down to the day before I had to move, yet I had no place to go. When my three daughters came to help me finish packing, practically everything except the furniture had been packed and organized neatly in the garage. They helped me finish the last items and clean the place. We made a plan for them to come back with some male friends at ten o'clock the next morning to help me move. When I considered getting a truck for the move, the answer to my heart was, *"No."* Since my children are somewhat used to me being a little different in the way I do things, they didn't press me for answers on the location of my new home. For that, I was very appreciative since I had no answer for them.

By the grace of God, I never lost my trust that somehow God had a plan for me, and it was going to work out for good.[211] In order not to lose that trust, I had to keep resisting doubt and nervousness and keep believing that I was indeed hearing and following Him. Around eight o'clock I hinted to the Lord, "They're coming! What's the plan?" No answer! Finally, about ten o'clock, the Spirit of the Lord spoke to my heart to call the manager and ask if I could pay a proportional amount to keep my things in the garage for two weeks. They were a new management company, and I had only met the manager once at which time she had given me her number. I figured the office was closed that day, but I called anyway. To my surprise, she answered and agreed to the plan. It turned out the number she had given me was her cell phone!

When help arrived and they asked where to put the furniture, I told them to put it in the garage. What an easy move! Then I went to my daughter's home and relaxed in their guest bedroom. Afterwards, as I sought the Lord for my new place, He simply said, *"I have prepared a place for you."* I would soon find out that He certainly had.

My new place turned out to be the two bedroom home of the duplex connected to my three bedroom home! When the Lord told me to move, I had no clue that I would move next door. The former tenants had recently moved out, and it was not yet ready for a new occupant, so I stayed with my daughter for a month while they fixed it up. They even transferred my deposit without requiring the increased amount.

On moving day, we simply walked my belongings a few feet from the packed garage into my new place. It truly was my easiest move ever!

I came to understand that this was a good experience for me to practice keeping my joy during a test of faith and patience.[212] In former times, I had failed to pass tests that called for me to stay joyful and remain in faith while waiting on God. What a relief to finally pass this one!

He then showed me that since I stayed with it until the end, I received more than an answer to a need. I had pressed into another level of trust in Him. That is, I received a spiritual increase that doesn't come any other way. As I thought about that, I realized my trust level had indeed increased! It has become easier to relax and stay steady when things don't look like they're going to work out. Instead of fighting fear, I stay assured that the answer will come just like the Word promises. My capacity to trust the Lord has been stretched, and I'm glad to say it's been stretching more ever since.

> *I received a spiritual increase that doesn't come any other way.*

Hebrews 10:23 KJV says:

> *"Let us hold fast the profession of our faith without wavering; (for he is faithful that promised;)"*

The only way that I know to hold fast to faith without wavering is to be in constant fellowship with the Lord, receiving His peace and guidance–while thanking, praising, and worshiping Him and spending time in the Word and in His Presence. As we fellowship, we receive confirmation of His leading and we receive His strength to endure.[213]

The warnings we are given in the New Testament about what we will face in these end times clarifies why our faith is so necessary to overcome troubles and remain faithful to our Lord.[214] By our faith we stand strong so we won't become subject to the pressures and evil schemes of our enemy, which will escalate in these last days before Jesus returns.[215] Because of this, I believe we must grow our faith and increase our trust in the Lord in order to overcome whatever we face now and in the days ahead. When Jesus comes, we pray He will find many who live by faith and stand strong for Him, and I'm working on being one of them.

STAY FAITHFUL TO THE END

> *There will be so much more evil in the world that
> the love of most believers will grow cold. But the
> one who remains faithful to the end will be saved.*
> (Matthew 24:12-13 ERV)

Over the years, I have witnessed many Christians who fail to remain faithful to God even after expressing a heartfelt confession of their desire and intent to give all to Him. Somewhere down the line, they would fall short and go back to their old lifestyles and bondages.

We were concerned for a loved one who sternly confessed that he was done with going backwards and stumbling around in sin, and yet he did. My daughter asked, "Why do they go back?" I told her that I couldn't say for sure, so we talked about a few reasons. Later on, when I thought about it again, the Lord spoke to my heart:

> *"They don't go far enough with Me to allow the
> Presence of God to replace those things that comfort
> and bind them."*

As I considered what He said, I knew He meant that the same bondages and addictions that once bound my loved ones were what they turned to for comfort when pressures arose. That is, they would go back to those bondages of alcohol, drugs, tobacco, etc, to relieve the pressures and temptations instead of drawing close to God to allow the satisfaction and joy in His Presence to fill their souls and drive away the darkness.[216] He gave me this Scripture as an answer:

> *...So we must once and for all strip away what
> is done in the shadows of darkness, removing*

*it like filthy clothes. And once and for all we
clothe ourselves with the radiance of light as our
weapon...Instead fully immerse yourselves into
the Lord Jesus, the Anointed One, and don't waste
even a moment's thought on your former identity to
awaken its selfish desires.* (Romans 13:12,14 TPT)

I recalled how the pressures of life and pressures from the
enemy against my mind tempted me to turn back at the beginning
of my Christian life. However, I had teachers who taught me
how to grow my faith and grow strong in the Lord.[217] I was also
empowered through studying the Bible and Biblical books to
replace my old bondages with His fellowship and Presence. In the
process of learning and growing, He has become my joy, my peace
and everything I need. And the Word of God has become my
daily spiritual food that strengthens me and keeps me increasing
in faith.[218]

Because I've personally known and prayed much for some
who have gone backwards in their walk with God, the Spirit of the
Lord spoke this Word to my heart on May 28, 2011:

*"My children–You who come to Me and give Me
your lives and then turn back in your hearts,
seeking for satisfaction apart from Me, and thereby,
eat the vomit of the putrid sin that I delivered you
from–I love you, and I want you to know the sweet
and satisfying refreshment of My love that cannot
be compared to the pleasures of sin that this world
offers.[219] I do not condemn you;[220] I reach to you. I
knock on your heart to remind you that I am yours.
Please open up to Me and let us sup together around
My Word.[221] Let My sweet Presence embrace you
and satisfy your soul so you will seek to love no*

other. Let Me have your whole heart like you have Mine.

Don't let your love grow cold because you are so distant from Me in your mind. Think on Me, and you will see that I am there for you always.[222] *Nothing can separate you from My love, but many things can separate Me from your love and cause you to grow lukewarm or even cold towards Me and eventually divorce Me in your heart.*

I will never divorce you, for I will never break our Covenant, but I cannot force you against your will not to divorce Me. Even if you do draw up the divorce papers and serve them to Me, I will never stop reaching out to you to return to Me, as long as you have breath in your body."

I pray every person who has turned away from the Lord will respond to God's love call and turn back to Him. May we all allow the Holy Spirit, our Helper, to work in us, for us and through us to honor the costly price Jesus paid to redeem us and restore us back to the Father. May we all be a part of the Family of God who will one day fill the Father's House.[223] May we make ourselves ready for our soon coming King!

And the Spirit and the bride say, "Come!" And let him who hears say, "Come!..." (Revelation 22:17 NKJV)

REFERENCES

1   Romans 8:37; Revelation 12:11

2   John 10:10; Matthew 26:41; Revelation 12:9; 2 Corinthians 2:11,14; Romans 8:35-37 AMPC

3   2 Peter 3:18

4   Matthew 6:33; Psalm 34:9-10

5   Isaiah 54:17; Psalm 91:10

6   1 Samuel 2:30

7   John 3:16-17; Romans 10:13; Acts 2:21; Matthew 9:29

8   Malachi 3:6; Isaiah 38:1-5; Acts 9:40

9   John 8:31-32

10   Joshua 24:15

11   Psalms 100:4; 22:3

12   John 16:13

13   John 3:17; Romans 8:1-2

14   1 John 3:20-21; Revelation 12:10

15   Hebrews 4:14-16; Luke 22:41-44

16   Colossians 2:15; Revelation 12:11; Romans 8:37

17   Romans 3:22-24; Colossians 1:27; Galatians 5:22-25; 1 Corinthians 12:1,7-11

18   Romans 14:10; 2 Corinthians 5:10; Jn 8:32

19   Romans 8:34; Hebrews 7:25

20   Isaiah 47:4

21   2 Peter 3:18; 2 Corinthians 4:13; James 1:21-27; Jude 20-21; Romans 1:17

22   Ephesians 5:26

23   2 Samuel 2:30

24   Luke 13:6-9

25   Psalms 51:17; 34:18

26   2 Chronicles 33:1-11 NLT

27   2 Chronicles 33:14-16 NLT
28   Isaiah 38:1-6
29   Jonah 1:1-2; 3:3-10
30   Revelation 2; 3
31   Matthew 7:1
32   Romans 8:26-27; 2 Corinthians 2:14; John 14:15,23; 1 Corinthians 10:13; Psalm 142:3 TPT
33   Philippians 4:6
34   Romans 8:37; Luke 10:19; Mark 16:17-18
35   Isaiah 53:3-5; 1 Peter 2:24
36   2 Corinthians 2:14; John 16:33
37   Romans 10:17; John 6:63; 16:12-15
38   Psalm 34:10; Philippians 4:19; Romans 5:2
39   Hebrews 11:6
40   John 16:23-24
41   James 1:5-8
42   James 2:17-26
43   Psalm 100
44   Matthew 6:9-13
45   2 Corinthians 1:20
46   James 1:5
47   Isaiah 55:11; Jeremiah 1:12
48   Luke 12:32
49   1 Timothy 6:12; Romans 10:17
50   John 10:10; 8:44
51   John 13:34;15:17; Romans:13:8; 1 Peter 4:8; Galatians 5:6
52   James 4:7-8; Psalm 16:11
53   2 Samuel 23:1; Acts 13:22
54   Exodus 20:3; Mark 12:30
55   Luke 13:11-16; Matthew 8:16; Acts 10:38
56   John 13:34;15:17; Romans 13:8; 1 Peter 4:8
57   Ephesians 4:27
58   Deuteronomy 4:19; 17:2-3
59   Ephesians 6:10-18; Jude 1:20; Hebrews 4:12; Ephesians 3:16
60   1 Peter 5:8-9
61   2 Thessalonians 3:16 NLT
62   Psalm 46:10 NLT
63   Colossians 3:15
64   Ephesians 6:10-18; 2 Corinthians 4:13

65   John 14:27; Philippians 4:6-8 NLT
66   Ephesians 4:27; 1 Peter 5:8
67   Proverbs 6:2; 10:19; 13:3
68   Mark 11:23
69   James 4:7
70   2 Corinthians 4:13
71   Isaiah 53:3-5; Matthew 8:16-17; 1 Peter 2:24
72   James 4:17
73   Psalm 141:3; Proverbs 16:9
74   2 Corinthians 4:13; James 2:26
75   Matthew 4:1-11
76   Romans 8:37; Mark 16:16-19; Luke 10:19; Colossians 2:15; 2 Corinthians 4:13
77   Ephesians 6:10-13; 1 Peter 5:9; James 4:7
78   Ephesians 6:17; 2 Corinthians 10:4
79   Ch 1, "Stay in Faith and Don't Doubt"
80   2 Corinthians 10:3-6; Ephesians 5:26
81   John 14:30 AMPC
82   Psalm 91:1-2; Ephesians 6:10-18
83   Revelation 12:11
84   Hebrews 3:1; 4:14-16; 10:23
85   1 John 3:8b
86   Romans 5:5; Ephesians 3:16; 2 Thessalonians 3:3 AMP; Psalm 119:165 TPT; Philippians 4:13
87   1 John 3:10-15
88   Ephesians 4:27; 2 Corinthians 2:10-11
89   2 Timothy 1:7
90   2 Corinthians 4:13; Mark 11:22-24
91   Amos 3:3; Hebrews 1:3
92   Psalms 8:1-2; 9:1-3
93   John 17:17
94   Romans 8:37; John 16:33
95   See Chapter 3, Generational Fear
96   Jeremiah 1:12; Isaiah 55:11
97   1 Peter 5:8; John 10:10
98   John 8:32; 2 Peter 1:2-4; 3:18
99   2 Corinthians 2:11; 1 Peter 5:8-9
100 Proverbs 20:7; 11:21; 14:26; 22:6; Psalms 102:28; 112:2; Isaiah 54:13; 44:3
101 1 Peter 5:8

102   Galatians 3:13-14, 29; James 4:7
103   Isaiah 54:13-14; 61:3
104   1 John 3:8
105   Luke 10:10; James 4:7; Mark 16:17
106   1 Peter 5:8-9; Ephesians 6:10-12
107   Luke 10:19; 2 Corinthians 11:3
108   John 10:10
109   2 Corinthians 2:11
110   Isaiah 61:3
111   Ephesians 4:27
112   See Ch 1, "Close the Door on the Enemy"
113   1 John 3:8; 2 Timothy 4:18
114   John 10:10
115   2 Corinthians 10:4-5; James 4:7
116   2 Corinthians 2:11; 1 Peter 5:8-9; Ephesians 4:27
117   Luke 13:16; Acts 10:38
118   Luke 9:1; 10:17-19; Isaiah 53:3-5; 1 Peter 2:24
119   John 13:34; 15:12,17; Romans 13:9; 1 John 3:23; 4:21; 2 John 1:5-6
120   Matthew 12:25; Luke 11:17
121   1 John 4:8; 3:21-23; 1 Peter 3:7
122   Ephesians 4:27; 2 Corinthians 2:11
123   Matthew 18:18; Hebrews 1:14
124   2 Corinthians 2:10-11; Ephesians 4:26-27; James 3:16
125   Mark 16:17; Luke 10:19; 1 John 3:8b
126   Proverbs 26:2
127   John 16:33
128   Ephesians 6:17; Psalm 149:6; Revelation 1:16; 12:11
129   Psalms 145:8-9; 23:6; Lamentations 3:22-23; Hebrews 10:23; 2 Timothy 2:13; John 3:16-17
130   John 10:10
131   Romans 8:31-37
132   Jeremiah 29:11; Ephesians 2:10; John 10:10; 2 Corinthians 2:14
133   John 1:14
134   Acts 20:28; Leviticus 17:11
135   1 John 1:7; Ephesians 2:13; Romans 3:24-25; 5:9 NLT; Hebrews 9:14; 10:22 ERV
136   Nehemiah 8:10; Psalm 16:11
137   Proverbs 17:22
138   2 Peter 3:18

139 Revelation 2:4-5
140 Ephesians 6:16; 1 Timothy 6:12
141 2 Corinthians 10:4; Matthew 4:1-11
142 Hebrews 12:1-3 TPT
143 John 16:33 AMPC
144 Isaiah 53:3-5 AMPC; 1 John 3:8; 1 Peter 2:24
145 1 Timothy 6:12; Romans 8:37; 1 Corinthians 15:57
146 Mark 16:18; 6:13; Acts 9:12; James 5:14-16; Romans 10:10; James 1:21
147 Ch 2, "Speak the Word Faithfully"
148 1 John 3:8b
149 Hebrews 10:23; 1 Peter 5:8-9; James 4:7
150 Ephesians 1:3; 2 Peter 1:3-4; 1 Peter 2:24; Colossians 1:12-14
151 Ch 2, "Speak the Word Faithfully"
152 2 Corinthians 4:13
153 Ch 2, "Speak The Word Faithfully"
154 Ezekiel 47:12; Revelation 22:2-3
155 "Adult Dehydration," K Taylor, EB Jones; ncbi.nlm.nih.gov/books/ NBK555956/
156 Ephesians 5:6-21; Hebrews 12:1
157 2 Corinthians 7:1; 2 Timothy 2:21; Ephesians 5:25-27; Hebrews 9:14
158 Revelation 19:7-8; 22:12,17, 20-21
159 Matthew 25:14-30; 2 Corinthians 5:9-10; Romans 14:10-12
160 1 Corinthians 6:19-20; 1 Peter 1:14-19
161 John 15:12, 17; Galatians 5:14; Ephesians 4:32; Romans 12:9-10; 1 John 3:11,14-18; 4:16, 20-21
162 Galatians 3:11-14; John 17:20-23;1 Peter 1:13-19; 1 John 5:4-5; Ephesians 4:1-32; Romans 12:21
163 Matthew 25:21 NKJV
164 Revelation 22:12; 20:11-15; Ephesians 6:8; 2 Corinthians 5:9-10; 1 Corinthians 3:9-15; Romans 14:10-12
165 2 Corinthians 2:14 AMPC
166 Hebrews 12:1-3
167 Romans 8:31-37; 2 Peter 1:2-4; John 16:13; Galatians 5:16-25; Hebrews 1:14
168 John 1:16-17 AMPC; 2 Corinthians 12:9; Matthew 11:28-30; 1 John 5:3
169 2 Corinthians 13:5; Galatians 6:4; Romans 12:1-2
170 Ephesians 6:4
171 1 Corinthians 11:31-32; 1 John 1:9; Revelation 2:4-5; 2 Timothy 2:21
172 John 16:13-14; Romans 8:14

173   Proverbs 8:11; 16:16
174   1 Corinthians 1:24, 30
175   Luke 12:32; Matthew 6:33; 1 Peter 5:7
176   Luke 18:8 NKJV
177   Matthew 11:28-30; Hebrews 4:9-11
178   2 Thessalonians 3:16; John 14:27
179   1 Corinthians 2:9-10; Ephesians 2:10; Jeremiah 29:11
180   John 8:32; Isaiah 55:8-11
181   Mark 6:6
182   1 John 3:8b
183   John 10:10
184   Galatians 5:19-21; Luke 21:34-36; 1 John 5:21; 2 Corinthians 7:1
185   Proverb 4:23 NLT
186   1 John 3:20-22; Hebrews 4:16
187   Romans 8:5-8; Psalm 97:10; Proverbs 8:13; 6:16-19; Amos 5:15
188   Psalm 119:11
189   Psalm 16:11; Hebrews 1:3; 4:12
190   Ephesians 6:10; Philippians 4:13
191   2 Corinthians 12:9
192   1 John 5:3
193   John 5:19,30; 14:16
194   Philippians 4:13
195   Revelation 19:7-8
196   Romans 8:14; 2 Corinthians 2:14; Matthew 13:43; Revelation 2:7,11,17,29
197   John 17:20-24; 11:41-42
198   Romans 12:1-2; 2 Corinthians 2:16
199   Romans 13:11-14;
200   1 Peter 2:11; 2 Corinthians 7:1 NLT
201   2 Peter 2:19
202   Hebrews 12:1
203   Isaiah 60:1-2
204   Ephesians 5:25-27
205   Romans 12:1-2
206   Revelation 19:7
207   Isaiah 46:10; Psalms 97:9-10; 138:1-2; Isaiah 33:10,13
208   1 John 3:8; Colossians 2:14-15
209   Hebrews 10:12-13; Revelation 12:10-11
210   Colossians 3:15
211   Romans 8:28

212 James 1:2-4
213 Proverb 3:6; Romans 4:20-21; John 10:27; 2 Corinthians 2:14; John 16:13-15; Ephesians 6:10 AMP
214 Matthew 24:3-14; 2 Timothy 3:1-8; Jude 1:14-19
215 2 Corinthians 1:24; Romans 11:20
216 Psalms 16:11; 8:1-2; 9:1-3
217 Ephesians 6:10
218 2 Thessalonians 1:3
219 2 Peter 2:20-22
220 John 3:17
221 Revelation 3:20
222 Hebrews 12:1-2
223 John 14:2-3

Printed in the United States
by Baker & Taylor Publisher Services